The Dynamics and Contradictions of an Evangelisation in Africa

The Dynamics and Contradictions of Evangelisation in Africa

An Essay on the Kom Christian Experience

Peter Acho Awoh

Langaa Research & Publishing CIG
Mankon, Bamenda

Publisher:
Langaa RPCIG
Langaa Research & Publishing Common Initiative Group
P.O. Box 902 Mankon
Bamenda
North West Region
Cameroon
Langaagrp@gmail.com
www.langaa-rpcig.net

Distributed outside N. America by African Books Collective
orders@africanbookscollective.com
www.africanbookscollective.com

Distributed in N. America by Michigan State University Press
msupress@msu.edu
www.msupress.msu.edu

ISBN: 9956-578-21-5

© Peter Acho Awoh 2011

DISCLAIMER

All views expressed in this publication are those of the author and do not necessarily reflect the views of Langaa RPCIG.

Content

Acknowledgment xii
Preface xiii
Foreword xvii

Chapter One: Introduction

Background to German Annexation 2
Early Missionary Manoeuvres in Cameroon 3
Evangelisation and Early History 6
Kom Early History 9
German Colonisation and Christianity 14
Evangelisation Under the British 16
The Sacred Heart Missionaries in Kom 18
African Chrisitanity in Retrospect 20
Colonial and Missionary Motives 21
Catholicism and African Traditional Religion 23
Philosophical and Cultural Consequences of Conversion
  to Christianity 25
Evangelisation and Conversion Models 28
Christian Villages and Early Converts to Christianity 31
The Triple Heritage and Shattered Dreams 35

Chapter Two: Missionary Theology

Introdction 41
Apostolic and Patristic Times 41
Magisterial Teaching 13th Century to the 15th Century 45
Age of Exploration, Discovery and Colonisation 46
Vatican II Era 51
Polemics and Controversies Since Vatican II 54

v

Chapter Three: Motives and Methods

Introduction 71
Missionary Methods 72
    Apostlic and Patristic Era 72
Mediaval Age 75
The Age of Exploration and Colonisation 76
Motives of Conversion to Christianity 80
    Introduction 80
Apostolic and Patristic Era 81
The Reformation 82
Age of Exploration and Colonisation 83
The Kom Christian Experience of Evangelisation 85
The Post War Era 87
Traditional Authorities and the Christianity in Conflict 89
Further Expansion of Christianity in Kom 93
Indigenous Missionary Initiatives 94
Missionary Tactics and Manoeuvres 97

Chapter Four: Present Day Challenges

Introduction 111
Subtle Anti Christian Literature and the Phenomenon
    of Reversion 113
Calls and Importance of Inculturation 117
    The Cultural Dialogue in the Patristic Era and
        the Middle Ages 120
    The Sixteenth-Century Evangelization of the American
        Indians 121
    Inculturation in the Far East 121
Criteria of Inculturation 122
    Christological Criterion 122
    Ecclesiological Criterion 122
    Anthropological Criterion 123

African Attempts at Inculturation 124
Possible Areas of Inculturation 127
Traditional and Christian Funeral Rites 127
Traditional Funneral Rites 130
Traditional Femine Rites 137
African and Christian Religious Underpinnings of
    Funneral Rites and Points of Divergence and
    Convergence 140
African Forms of Healing 151
    Introduction 151
Iking I Wayn 151
Ise 156
Origin and Purpose 156
Initiation and Purpose 157
African Spiritual World, Sickness, Healing and
    the Teaching of the Church 159
The Sacramental Rites 162
    Rite of Christian Initiation of Adults and Demonology 162
The Church's Faith in Healing Today 164
Fertility Rites 165
Fertility Rites in the Ancient Near East 167
Traditional Days of Obligations 168
    Origin and Purpose 168
Christian Days of Obligation 169
    Origin And Purpose 169
Traditional Concept and Practice of Justice 170
Conclusion 171

Selected Bibliography 181

To my dear beloved mother, Nawain Veronica Mai

Acknowledgment

In carrying out this project, I leaned heavily on several individuals, too many to enumerate and to whom I owe a great debt of gratitude. However, I must render my fervent thanks to the Brother Superior of the Marist District of West Africa, Rev. Brother Yao Sylvain kouassi Kan, FMS, who personally encouraged me to move on when fatigue and discouragement set in.

I must render my immense gratitude to Fr. John Musi Yonghabi who personally provided from his personal archives vital material whose absence would have greatly improvised this work. Worthy of mention is Dr. Ndongmanji John who personally went out of way to proofread countless number of times the manuscript. I remained very grateful to Fr. Maurice McGill, Fr. Jude Thaddeus Mbi, Br. Jean Baptist Tamessuien, Br. Martin Nguma Mbeng, Br. Kpunsa Stephen, Br. Nyuydine John ,Br. Lukong Francis, Br.Tata Oliver, Sr. Kiven Linda and Sr. Kelly Dorothy.

I owe a debt of gratitude to Dr. Anthony Ndi Mbunwe who willingly accepted to write the preface at short notice. Immense thanks to the Sr. Doris kongla, Sr. Hedwig Vinyo and Sr. Assumpta Dzmendze of the Tertiary Sisters of St Francis of La Verna Community, Foncha street, Nkwen. They generously provided an enabling environment for my ideas to blossom.

I remained indebted to my twin brother and friend, Awoh Paul Ngwain, who actively was involved in collecting the necessary resources on the ground. Special thanks to Mr. Yong Charles Toh and students of GBHS Fundong who contributed useful resources from their personal lived experiences. Many thanks to my Dad, Bobe Awoh Blasius Maindu, for his paternal encouragement and admonition. Lastly but not the least, to Bobe Marcus Nkwi catechist of Njinikom, Bobe Andrew Nkuna Timti and Bobe Nkfum Mformie, who were very instrumental in shaping certain sections of this work.

Preface

Generally, missionary enterprise is rightly or wrongly associated with the colonial era, which ended in Cameroon as in most African countries in the 1960^s. In fact, the Cameroon Baptist Convention (CBC) declared independence from the Cameroon Baptist Mission (CBM) in 1954, while the Presbyterian Church in Cameroon (PCC), in the same manner secured autonomy from the Basel Mission (BM) in 1957. The Roman Catholic Mission (RCM) on the other hand, changed hands following the Episcopal ordination of Local Ordinaries in the Bamenda and Buea dioceses in 1970 and 1971 transforming itself from the RCM to the 'Catholic Church' (CC).

In a way, therefore, it could logically be argued that these excision processes concluded the missionary era in West Cameroon by 1972. Indeed, in terms of authority, structures, and conspicuous missionary presence in the field, this could be true, but missionary legacy is profound, complex, fascinating and has continued to engage much more than just academic interest and fantasy. This is because the contributions made and the challenges raised by missionary activity in Cameroon in particular, Africa and elsewhere, physically, psychologically and spiritually were enormous, dynamic and penetrating. Missionary impact is therefore an indelible part of our history.

Early accounts on the work of these intrepid 'warriors for Christ' were documented by a few of the missionary writers themselves but the task has since fallen into the hands of products of that enterprise themselves. There has been an influx of publications tackling that experience from various perspectives by beneficiaries or receivers, who proclaim missionary history from their own lived experience.

Brother Peter Awoh's work can best be appreciated in this context. He tackles the subject using a broadly, engaging and an all-encompassing approach; combining historical, theological, philosophical, liturgical and socio-cultural concepts of the missionary enterprise in Kom. In short, the Kom (African) mind is placed within the wider framework of Church History. He raises serious concerns about the motivation and sustenance of missionary interests and how profoundly these have been received and grounded in the Kom (African) Christian culture, and proceeds to make suggestions for meaningful inculturation. This work would certainly interest various formation houses and religious institutes, where it could generate further meaningful discussion and debate on missiology.

Dr. Anthony Ndi Mbunwe
Foncha Street Bamenda
April 2010

Foreword

Almost a century has gone by since the first band of Sacred Heart Missionaries from Germany ventured into the Kom highlands. It was a journey of faith, a faith founded on the theology of the time, which provided the zeal for these men to abandon family and country. They were men according to modern standards ill equipped for the Herculean task ahead of them. In a spirit of resignation, they were convinced that unless the lord builds the house in vain do the labourers labour.

Taking advantage of the normalisation of relations between the Church and state in Germany, the Sacred Heart Missionaries at the invitation of the Pallotine Missionaries arrived Cameroon, made their way gradually into the remote areas of the kom highlands, and settled in Fujua, a few kilometres from Laikom, the seat of the Fon of Kom. While their contemporary compatriots were searching for areas to invest capital and reap corresponding profit even at the cost of their own lives and those of natives, these band of men were in search of souls to sow the seed of the word of God who were in the thought of the time heading to perdition on a daily basis in large numbers. The lofty ambitions, which lurked in the hearts of these men of God, were suddenly crushed with the internment order issued by the allied forces, which effectively brought to an end the activities of all German nationals in the territories including missionaries.

Many traditional rulers thought they had seen the last of the Whiteman's religion. Their celebration was premature as they saw their hopes dashed by the return of Christians. This native, militant, resurgent and resilient brand of Christianity brewed in the far distant island of Fernando Po was mainly made up of ex soldiers who had been schooled on the rubrics of Catholicism. It was this small band of Christians, small in numbers but strong in determination, that resisted all attempts from the Traditional Authorities to crush the seed of Christianity.

This vibrant band of Christians who had returned from Fernando Po did not for obvious reasons returned to care for the reins of the buildings left behind by the departing missionaries of the Sacred Heart

Missionary Order. It is for this reasons that Fujua the cradle of Christianity in kom gradually sank into oblivion. Between the departure of the Sacred Heart Missionaries and the advent of the Mill Hill Missionaries the Christian faith was sustained by Christians who were missionaries to their own compatriots. It was the missionaries of St. Joseph Society for Foreign Missions who were later to give the Church its character and to pilot the Church into the future.

The missionary motives of the first missionaries were founded on the prevailing thought patterns of the time, which were based on the belief that salvation was only possible within the Catholic Church, and whoever was outside the visible confines of the Catholic Church was on the road to perdition. It was this sympathetic move to save the rest of humanity from perdition that galvanised the missionaries into action into areas even where their lives were in jeopardy. West and central Africa had lived up to its reputation as the Whiteman's grave. With fewer and fewer missionaries returning to their home countries, one would have advised caution with a high percentage of them falling prey to disease in the disease infested tropics. The desire to save the African souls, even at the cost of their own lives, drove the missionaries into the interior that no land was too remote to escape their attention and vigilance. This strong belief in the worth of every human soul and the desire to save it from eternal damnation was what kept missionary zeal buoyant through out the centuries leading missionaries to abandon home and country. The clarification of the concept of salvation within the Church during the Vatican II Council set in motion the current lethargy that has in some places crippled mission itself.

It is almost a century since the first missionaries criss-crossed the nooks and crannies of this country. Some of the areas they visited are still undergoing primary evangelisation. With the current though about mission in several quarters casting doubts on mission Ad Gentes itself, one can almost say that succeeding missionaries have in some areas trailed the same paths their forbearers trailed without venturing into unexplored areas.

It is now close to a century of evangelisation and enough time for one to assess with hindsight the fruits of this missionary endeavour. In retrospect, one can begin to wonder why people became Christians. What reasons motivated the early adherents to cling to this foreign religion. Were there some deficiencies in African Traditional Religion, which the Africans hope to remedy by joining the new religion or it was just part of the wholesale flirting with whatever was western? Those who sided with these missionaries often paid a price by cutting themselves off from the traditional network of social security. Christianity was a danger to many of the time-honoured solutions to African problems, to traditional systems, rites, and rituals, which represented the utilitarian feature of African Traditional Religion. Christianity in many cases true to the culture of the time was not interested in a theological dialogue with the African Traditional Religion. This was a recipe for the reversion to some traditional practices, which the African could not avoid in time of crisis. A phenomenon, which has persisted into the modern times.

Missionary activity was initiated and kept alive in many areas not only by those who are refereed to as missionaries in the true sense of the word but by the remnant of the ex soldiers who had returned from Fernando Po and in later years by Christians who had moved away from the stronghold of Christianity in Njinikom to other areas. From its inception, Christianity seemed very harmless and for sure, missionaries worked in ways than can almost be termed insidious. For many Africans, their coming into the Whiteman's Church was part of the general flirting with the Whiteman's enterprise of colonial emancipation. Missionaries themselves shrewdly avoided presenting this lethal aspect of Christianity. With the return of the ex soldiers from Fernando Po, the ensuring conflict and the Mass exodus of the Fon's wife, it became clear that Christianity had in its bosom some elements which threatened certain facets of African Traditional Religion. The wrath of traditional authorities against Christians all over the entire Fondom resulted in outright persecution of Christians. In areas where a Christian enclave strong enough to shelter them had not been created, Christians were forced to operate under the guise of a dancing group. This phenomenon was generally evolved as the modus vivendi and modus operandi. The number of Christians who suffered persecution is not negligible and it will be left to succeeding generations of

Christians to immortalise them as the early martyrs have been immortalised in the universal Church. One can rightly say that the first page of the martyriology and why not santology has already been written with the lives and blood of the first Christians.

The growth and expansion of Catholicism into areas out of Njinikom was at a time when Christianity had begun to loose some of its initial flavour and fervour. It encountered Christians who had fallen away from the faith. With the admonition of a missionary who might have encountered them in their religious indifference and stupor, some of these lax or fall away Christians became the axis on which new Christian communities were to revolve. It also witnessed a turnabout in missionary policy. Initially the Christian community at Njinikom had the project of the Church realised thanks to the support of the entire population. This cordial relation soon ruptured when the Fon was incensed by the blatant affront to his authority and Mass exodus of his wives. In years to come the compounds of the Quarter Heads, the guarantors of the traditional practices, were the very entry points for the establishment of Christianity in many villages. The visit to the chief or Quarter Head of a specific locality by a missionary on his first visit was as a matter of policy the method used by missionaries. After close to century of Christian experience one can begin sift with hindsight what might have been done in another way.

With the waning of the initial fervour of Christianity the phenomenon of reversion began to appear. A number of Christians began to fall away from the faith or simply decided to harbour the old and the new. Which is the way forward for the second century of Christianity? The Post-Synodal Apostolic Exhortation Ecclesia in Africa on the Church in Africa and its Evangelizing Mission towards the year 2000 highlighted this disturbing phenomenon. Inculturation was proposed as the way forward. Many of the attempts made so far in the inculturation process have been in the area of song and dance which falls immediately in the liturgy of the Church. What so far has remained almost untouched is the area of theological inculturation. It is incumbent on the Church to shed light and convincingly overcome any doubts or ambiguity in areas where the gospel message and the African Traditional Religion conflict.

It is true that Christianity has always been a sign of contradiction, responsible for the raising and falling of many cultures and systems in the past, in the present and so it will be in the future. If the Christian message, which is always, countercultural remains so today, it is only true to its nature. From the beginning, Christianity has always posed a threat to some established order. If it does not do so or has ceased to do so one can have no doubt about the compromise it has made. The best actors in this dialogue are the African Christians themselves who have fully imbibed the spirit of Christ and can examine African cultural values with the same spirit. The possible areas of inculturation are many but some are more urgent and prominent than others. Some of them include honour paid to the dead, eschatology, sin, sickness and healing, traditional days of obligation, and traditional concepts of justice among others. While some reflections have been offered in this sphere, it is up the Church to make them alive in this dialogue.

One can almost say with certainty that the experience of the early Christians and the reaction of the established world order of the time was re-enacted in many ways in this milieu. From Pentecost to the martyrdom of Stephen, from the martyrdom to the movement out of Jerusalem, and more vividly up to the edict of Milan Christianity was seen as subversive because of the threats it posed to the established order of the time both religious and civil. In the African setting, it posed even a greater danger to the time honoured solutions to African problems, which had stood the test of time and formed the very foundations on which ethnic groups were built. African Traditional Religion is highly utilitarian. African Traditional Religion is concerned mainly with saving and safeguarding life. What may be considered sin in Christian theology especially against the first three precepts of the Decalogue, for the adherents of African Traditional Religion are some of those solutions to problems, which threaten life, and Africans regularly resort to them to save life. The decisive test of religion is man's behaviour in a crisis. What he does when stirred up to the very depths of his being, when he is racked with pain, when his crops fail, that constitutes his religion.[1] It is certain that the African will stop at nothing to save life even if the

---

1. Robert Lowie: An introduction to Cultural Anthropology, London 1934, p. 304.

means contravenes the first and second precepts of the Decalogue. Many well placed Christians believe that all traditional institutions have good intentions but the devil is attempting to use them for personal gains. When Christianity frowns at some of these traditional institutions, some accused it of refusing to recognise the unknown god in the words of Paul in Athens.[2]

A thorough analysis of the African Traditional Religion with its different forms of expression from honour paid to the dead, fertility rites, concept of justice, taboos, soothsaying to necromancy among others leaves no one in doubt that the reason is to safeguard life and make it more comprehensible. The eradication of these 'values' became the object of missionary preaching. This is one of the reasons why Christianity was distrusted from the beginning and Mass adult conversions were not the norm. From resistance to this attempt to erode what was seen as the core of identity of the African, the phenomenon of reversion and compromise can almost be said to have been the way for some Christians. The line dividing the Christian from non-Christian, which was very visible in the past, has become blurred over the years.

Any meaningful way forward will have to convincingly overcome and defeat any doubts about the efficacy of Christianity to fill the void which a true and radical conversion to Christianity unavoidably create in communities and the lives of individuals. After almost close to a century after the first wave of primary evangelisation the percentage of Christians in the general population leaves no one in doubt that only a small percentage of the population has become Christian. The early conversions to Christianity were because of miracles and the preaching of the apostles, the expansion of Christianity into areas of Europe was a result of many factors besides faith in Jesus and the eternal salvation. In the early history of missionary work in this part of the world, conversions were not in response to any miracles worked by the missionaries, schools in many cases became nurseries of Christian Churches. At a time when confessional schools are not the only schools in the neighbourhood and with attendance of Catholic Christian children in Catholic schools dwindling one can almost say if the new wave of

---

2. Cf Bochong Chia Francis Ngam: A Christian Discourse presented to the Catholic Christians in Fundong Parish. p.12.

evangelisation is to bear fruits the Church has to be more creative in the way the gospel is proclaim and as well as the avenues which have traditionally been used to proclaim the Good News. The traditional pattern has been that the new Christians have mainly been children of Christians and the conversions of non-Christians have not been the norm. It is time the Church should borrow not only the methods but also the zeal with which the first missionaries proclaim the Good News to our Fathers some years ago.

Peter Acho Awoh
St. Albert's Comprehensive College
Bafut
April 2010

CHAPTER ONE

INTRODUCTION

The third phase of Africa's systematic evangelization began in the nineteenth century, a period marked by an extraordinary effort organized by the great apostles and promoters of the African mission. It was a period of rapid growth[1]. The nineteenth century witnessed unprecedented changes on a global scale, which hitherto had not been witnessed by humanity. These changes affected virtually every sphere of life. There was hardly a place on the earth's surface that was left unaffected by this sudden global surge in exploration manoeuvres. Between 1870 and 1900, and especially after 1885, a sudden and striking change occurred in the relations between Europe and the rest of the world. In these years, the last and most spectacular attempt by Europe to dominate the world was made. No one possible explanation can account for this sudden desire for colonies.

European countries became industrialised and new markets for their products had to be found. Colonies provided not only a new market but also a source of raw materials. Imperialism – the quest for colonies began as a search for new markets and an increase in wealth. As Europe became a world power with a network of political and economic interest around the globe, rivalries among European states intensified transforming most of them into armed camps. This, combined with the growing feelings of nationalism, imperialistic and militaristic impulses, created an atmosphere that eventually led to strife and dissension.

Before 1875, the common wisdom was that colonies brought both benefits and problems to a modern state, but after that year western thinking abruptly changed. Europe's industrialised states began to compete for colonies and for trade rights around the world. To maintain their high standards of living, they had to find new markets, underdeveloped areas, where to invest capital as well as cheap sources of raw materials. Given these needs, the continent of Africa became the final destination of imperialistic ambition of western nations.

As late as 1850, people still spoke of Africa as the Dark Continent. By 1914, the entire continent except for Abyssinia and Liberia had been divided up among the European nations. In the middle of the century the bravery of explorers like the Scottish missionary, Dr. Livingstone among many others opened up the centre of Africa to western influence and control. Very quickly, the main European powers began to seize portions of these lands as colonies and to claim surrounding territories as their spheres of influence.

BACKGROUND TO GERMAN ANNEXATION

It was purely an affair of certain countries and Germany under Bismarck refused to be entangled in this craze for colonies. Not only did he believe that Germany's interest lay in Europe but he was also anxious not to provoke Britain unnecessarily. The creation of a German naval force would have attracted the wrath of Britain. Bismarck was unwilling to upset this delicate balance of power. It was for this reason that Germany stood aloof maintaining a safe distance from the squabbles emanating from the friction among European powers in quest for colonies. To gain colonies would mean a German navy, a thing, which would not be welcomed by Britain.

However, events proved too strong for him. Pressure on him came from the German African Society formed in 1878 and the German colonial league, which was formed four years later in 1882.Both organizations, urged Bismarck to make claims in Africa as other nations had done. Unfortunately for Bismarck his reign saw the expansion of the German industry, the population of Germany increased by 43 per cent, the building of the railway encouraged rural urban migration, more and more Germans began to cross the Atlantic and to open up trade with the middle and the Far East. Bismarck was not keen on entering the colonial race largely because he did not want to challenge Britain by sea. With all more and more prospects for prosperity it seemed to many Germans that there was no limit to what their nation could achieve. Bismarck had no option than to revise his ideas. It was this economic expansion which was to put Germany forward as a participant in the race for colonies overseas. Anxious at all cost not to upset this system of European alliances by offending other nations, Bismarck decided to call conferences in Berlin in November 1884 to discuss all the problems which the scramble for Africa was causing. Cameroon gradually came into focus as a German sphere of influence owing to the fact that German industrialist hungry for profit had already invested capital in Cameroon.

EARLY MISSIONARY MANOEUVRES IN CAMEROON

The history of evangelization in Cameroon is closely related to the history of colonization. As a whole the history of colonization and evangelization went hand in hand, in fact they became two strange bedfellows from the beginning. The evangelization of Cameroon started in 1840 when the first group of the Baptist missionaries landed in Cameroon all the way from Jamaica. It must be noted that from the beginning of evangelisation Cameroon was not a colony of any colonising European power. As time went on this leeway of missionaries in Cameroon from every nation was completely curtailed. Beginning with German annexation the history of evangelization was marked with controversy. Because of nationalistic tendencies, linguistic, denominational squabbles and schisms the missionary enterprise in Cameroon created obstacles that stood on the way of the mission they had set out to propagate. The protestant missionaries preceded the Catholic missionaries by almost half a century.

In the few years before the annexation of Cameroon by Germany, many British missionaries competed with the French to lure their countries to annex Cameroon. These took the form of letters written in the name of the local traditional authorities, requesting for annexation. In fact, Britain almost annexed Cameroon at the bidding of the missionaries. Only the late arrival of Hewett changed the course of colonial and missionary history of Cameroon once and for all.

The position of the German Government in Cameroon and in the colonies in general was influenced by the German foreign policy under Otto Von Bismarck. Bismarck, the German chancellor was responsible for the course of missionary action in Cameroon. He had a phobia and a general dislike for Jesuits and all that was Jesuit. This was the reason for the refusal to the request made by the Holy Ghost Fathers to set up a missionary post in Cameroon. For him all Catholic missionaries were more or less Jesuit in character and spirit.

However, with the passage of time the German government had to relax the conditions under which they would accept missionaries into their colonies. The missionaries had to be of German nationality, their superior had to be German and reside in Germany or a German controlled territory and their superiors were to refuse all directives and interference from outside.

The first Catholic Missionary Order to undertake the work of evangelisation in Cameroon, were the Pallotine Missionaries. It is important to examine the situation, which preceded their coming. Their coming was preceded by a great deal of controversy. The first Catholic Missionary Order that requested to work in Cameroon shortly after the German annexation were the French congregations of the Holy Ghost missionaries and the Holy Heart of Mary Immaculate. The German government refused to grant these Orders permission to establish in the territory for two reasons. First, because it was French and would work against German interest and second, because it had the Jesuit tendency of unquestionable and total obedience to their superiors.

In 1889 another Catholic Order, the Pallotine missionaries, requested to come over to Cameroon. After a very careful investigation and a thorough study of the Order's constitution, the government reluctantly granted permission. This came after Bismarck had visited East Africa and learned of the good work the Catholic missionaries were doing there. In granting the permission, the government had several conditions under which they were to operate in the colony. These conditions were that: The Basel mission should not object to their coming, only the German missionaries of the Order would be sent to the colony, the Order must keep out of the mission territory of the Basel mission, there must be no foreign control or interference in the Order's work in the colony, and the Order must use the German language in the colony. The Pallotines accepted these conditions and were ready to establish a Pallotine mission house and a training school in Limburg, in Germany. In 1890, the Basel mission removed their objections to Catholic missionaries coming to Cameroon, so long as they agreed to work only in regions not under their control. It is for this reason that the German Catholic missionaries did not follow the colonial authorities immediately. It took the German government close to six years to lift the objections and later the ban on Catholic missionaries in Cameroon, a ban which was lifted reluctantly and grudgingly under duress. Generally this was not the scenario. Through out history Catholic missionaries naturally followed their compatriots to the colonies. However, unlike most colonising European countries in the past, Germany had ceased to be predominantly Catholic. Not only was Germany not predominantly Catholic, it had institutionally evolved a subtle and sometimes open anti Catholic feeling.

As was the case with Asia and Latin America in the sixteenth century, the evangelization of Africa on a large scale was only possible in the era of the colonization of Africa. It was under these circumstances that German missionaries arrived in Cameroon. The German colonial enterprise in Cameroon served as a vehicle for the evangelization of the territory. The introduction of the German Pallotine Fathers and later the Sacred Heart Fathers in Cameroon was a direct consequence of German rule in Cameroon. It was in 1884 that the German formal annexation of Cameroon finally became a reality. However, behind the scenes missionaries in defiance to the national spheres of influence were eager to cast their nets into the deep. Applications from various Catholic missionary organizations to evangelise in Cameroon were systematically turned down until 1890 when the German government was forced to relent following the demise of Bismarck.

In 1883, a year before the German annexation of Cameroon two French missionaries of the Holy Ghost Fathers working in Gabon visited Cameroon with the aim of buying land to set up missionary stations. Shortly after the annexation of Cameroon in 1885 Nachtigal invited the French Holy Ghost Fathers to come to Cameroon. However, in 1885 with the arrival of Governor Von Soden, the romance ended abruptly on a sad note. The attempts to settle in Cameroon were futile. In November of the same year, Bismarck in a speech at the Reichstag categorically objected to the admission of the French missionaries in Cameroon.

The German foreign policy towards Catholic missions in Cameroon was a direct result of the turbulent relations with the Church in Germany. Following the declaration of papal infallibility, the German government became very unsure about the German Catholics whose allegiance to the papacy was too strong. If the pope said one thing and Bismarck disagreed, whom should a German Catholic obey? Bismarck at once saw that the claims of the pope could be a direct challenge to the all powerful state over which he ruled. The Vatican decrees stated that it was the duty of the state to enforce all decisions of the papacy.

In 1873, the government issued the May laws and other laws followed in the next two years. Following the May laws, the Jesuits, the great teaching Order of priests were expelled from Germany. No priest was allowed to inspect a school or a Church. Colleges had to have their examinations set by the state. The registration of births, marriages and deaths were taken out of the hands of the Church and given to state officers. Cardinals and Archbishops applauded by the congregations defied the law and went to prison. By 1870, some 1,300 parishes had no priests. However, following the growth of the Catholic Centre Party in the Reichstag and the coming of Pope Leo XIII, the May laws were withdrawn and Bismarck made peace with the new pope.

EVANGELISATION AND EARLY HISTORY

Following this normalisation in relations between the Papacy and Germany, in may 1889, the Sacred Congregation for the Propagation of Faith in Rome placed before the German government a memorandum of three points which included the availability of the German Pallotine Fathers to take over the evangelization of Cameroon, the creation of a new vicariate of Cameroon, and the consent of the Bishop of Munster to set up a mission centre in his Diocese for the Pallotine Fathers. In 1890 on the 18th of March, Rome created the apostolic prefecture of Cameroon and confided it to the Pallotine Fathers. In July of the same year Henri Vieter was nominated as First Prefect of Cameroon. In October, he and seven companions arrived in Cameroon. On the 8th of October 1890 the German Pallotine Fathers set up their first mission station at Marienburg and consecrated Cameroon to Mary, Queen of the apostles.[2]

At the invitation of the Pallotine missionaries, on the 28th of November 1912, missionaries of the Sacred Heart of Jesus arrived in the colony to cooperate with the Pallotine missionaries and to carry the Catholic faith into the interior and grasslands of Cameroon.

The Missionaries of the Sacred Heart of Jesus took over the station in Mamfe and opened another in Kom in July 1913. All over the world the practice whereby missionaries of different Orders tended to secure specific territories while keeping others out had almost became sacrosanct. To avoid squabbles emanating from differences in approach to mission policy it became incumbent on the missionaries to secure specific areas while jealously keeping others out. Partly this explains why the Sacred Heart Fathers concentrated on the interiors leaving the rest of the territories to other missionary Orders.

In 1884, Cameroon became a German protectorate, but since the Germans were primarily interested in the exploitation of the coastal areas, where climatic and soil conditions were favourable to plantation agriculture, the Grass fields escaped direct European penetration until the late 19th century. In 1889, Zintgraff, a German explorer, canvassed the area for economic resources potentially useful to Germany. In 1890, he visited Kom, where he met with outright hostility, but Kom had no further contact with Germans until 1901.[3] Following the defeat of the neighbouring tribe, Bafut, Fon Yu, congratulated the Germans on their victory over the Bafut people, and presented them with gifts and promises to supply labour for the new German military station in Bamenda. The apparent allegiance of Kom to the colonial rulers was short-lived. In 1904, Fon Yu rejected the German demands for labour, provoking a German military invasion of Kom

The German offensive was ruthless and bitter: Like the military tactics of the past, all villages on their path were burned down completely. Even the Kom palace at Laikom was occupied and later burnt. To further weaken and force the people to submission their means of sustenance that is the crops were destroyed.[4] Fon Yu went into hiding and after several months of battle, was persuaded in 1905 to sign a peace pact with the German aggressor, thereby placing Kom under German administration.[5] The gender imbalance of the population in Kom in the 1920s is testimony to the severity of the confrontation between the Germans and the Kom people: the men fled during the German offensive and died of cold and hunger.

After the subjugation of Kom in 1905, the relationship between Fon Yu and the German authorities seems to have been cordial. The head-tax, which was introduced in 1909, was paid regularly, and Kom supplied the porters and station labour demanded of it[6]. Kom young men were recruited into the German Schutztruppe as soldiers, messengers and carriers, providing the Germans with the information necessary for administration, and in 1908 a German military post was established at Njinikom.[7]

It was under these brutal, barbaric, and vicious circumstances that the third wave of evangelization began in earnest. Up to the 1800's though there were many religious institutes, which were missionary in outlook and character, Africa remained largely an unexplored area for them. The evangelization of China and Latin America was a natural consequence of colonialism. Jesuit missionaries who championed and pioneered primary evangelization of Asia and Latin America followed the ships of their own nations, which provided both the means and protection for their mission. When a Portuguese explorer sailed onto the shores of an island off the coast of India in 1500, eight Franciscans landed with him. The Spanish missionaries went in great numbers to the New World, following the explorers and soldiers whose purpose was conquest. Displaying a white standard ornamented with a purple cross of the divine Redeemer, the ships that transported the intrepid explorers bound for the western shores and islands of Africa carried missionaries. Henry, the Navigator supported the colonial and sacred expeditions, so the missionaries could subject the barbarians to the sweet yoke of Jesus Christ[8].

It was the same with the prince of Portuguese explorers, Vasco Da Gama who, weighing anchor to begin his fortunate trip to India, had with him two religious men of the Order of the Most Holy Trinity. One of them, after bringing the light of the gospel to India with apostolic zeal, suffered martyrdom. However, just as in all ages of the Church, so also at that time and in those far distant regions, the blood of this martyr and of the other heroic missionaries of Portugal became the seed of Christianity. Their illustrious example greatly inspired the Catholic world, including the spirited citizens of Portugal, to promote more widely the works of the apostolate[9].

The third phase of the introduction of Christianity in Africa represented by missionary activity, as from the nineteenth century saw the arrival of empire builders, explorers, missionaries, and traders simultaneously with colonial occupation, which contributed to the image of Christianity as one coloured by colonial rule. We are still very close to that period to dissociate ourselves from it. The years following the colonization of Africa saw the last of the unknown territories. These years also saw the missionaries of the Church following the newly blazed trails into the interior. One could rightly say that it was difficult to find an island remote enough to have escaped the vigilance and the energy of the missionaries. It is important to turn our attention to the land that was about to receive the faith. As we shall see, colonialism and Christianity combined into a lethal force whose effect was evident as the erosion of long standing cultural practices was set in motion. We will limit ourselves to some of the aspects that suffered the onslaught and bore the brunt of the double-edged sword of Christianity and colonialism. These two forces, though strange bedfellow often in antagonism, often at loggerheads and perpetually existing in acrimony were, in the eyes of some traditional authorities birds of the same feather with one ambition.

KOM EARLY HISTORY

The Kom kingdom in the Bamenda Grass fields occupies an area of about 280 square miles at an average altitude of about 5000 feet above sea level. The capital of Kom, Laikom, is located on a peak higher than 6000 feet above sea level. A high, grassy plateau, the Bamenda Grassfields region is characterized by a relatively high population density. The country is rugged and diverse, the highlands intersected by fertile valleys in which most of the settlements are found. The Grassfields are inhabited by five main population groups — the Tikar, Widekum, Mbembe, Bali and Aghem — as well as a small minority of Hausa and Fulani. Oral tradition links the Kom to the Tikar, who migrated from the Upper Mbam River and its tributaries prior to the eighteenth century. Linguistic and archaeological researches indicate a long, continuous occupation of the Bamenda highlands. Data pertaining to the early history of the Bamenda area suggest that the early Grassfield societies were not highly stratified. The typical political organization of the Grassfields was chiefdom, federating descent groups under the leadership of a Council or clan and lineage elders presided over by the Fon, a "primus inter pares."[10] Because of economic and political changes in the pre-colonial era, a number of strong, highly stratified, and centralized kingdoms, including Kom, emerged along the most important trade routes[11]

After the decrease of the legitimate Atlantic slave trade, the Grassfields supplied slave labour for the prospering palm oil plantations. According to Kaberry, the Kom kingdom was a major provider of slaves, obtained through raids and warfare. Increased trading activities in the 19th century laid the basis for the territorial expansion of Kom and the consolidation of its hegemony over smaller Grassfield chiefdoms. Kola, slaves, iron goods, guns, and livestock were the main goods traded by 19th century Kom traders. The expansion of trade resulted in an increase in social stratification, with a new social group emerging: merchants with large compounds and large numbers of wives. In general, the Grassfield economies were (and still are) characterized by a sharp gender division of labour according to a common sub-Saharan pattern: women perform subsistence farming and prepare food, while men perform income-generating activities, trade, clear bush and assist in the harvest.

In its political institutions, Kom resembles many neighbouring kingdoms and village chiefdoms, the main difference being that Kom is matrilineal, while most Grassfield kingdoms are patrilineal. The kingdom is traditionally ruled by a Fon, a powerful religious and secular leader[12], who is guided by Councils of advisors, and aided by numerous regulatory societies. As a divine ruler, the Fon is ascribed sacred qualities, and in the past, he exercised control over the life and death of his subjects. As an intermediary between his subjects and spirits of the past, the present, and the future, the Fon is vested with unquestioned authority in both spiritual and worldly matters. In the execution of his tasks a secret society, the Kwifon, and various personal advisors closely assist him. Conflict resolution is usually obtained through arbitration by Quarter Heads and Councillors, and the consultation of diviners.

A distinctive institution is the Kwifon, the executive arm of the Fon's government, endowed with advisory, judicial and ritual functions. Orders and messages from the Fon are communicated to the Kom people through Kwifon retainers. The Kwifon is a highly secretive body, organized in a hierarchy of lodges. Membership of its inner lodges was sharply restricted. In the execution of state duties, Kwifon officials appear clothed in net gowns which mask the face and body: its authority is of an impersonal kind, and its agents can not be held to account by the populace[13] The Kwifon not only executes orders of the Fon, but also regulated economic affairs, for example by inaugurating the harvest at a certain time and controlling the market. Duties of the Kwifon also include the recruitment of palace retainers from among freeborn commoners.

The Afoakom is the symbol of the kom people. These three figures in many ways reflect some biblical figures. The three men who visited Abraham under the sacred tree of Mamre in the book of Genesis 18: 2, three young men who were thrown into the blazing furnace in the book of Daniel 3;26 Shadrach, Meshack and Abednego. The motto of the people is food, child and prosperity. What is the spiritual significance of the number three? Christianity as well as Traditional African Religion make use of this significance number three in various ways.

The Fon stands very much apart from the rest of the populace, living in a large palace compound on the hilltop Laikom. He is regarded with infinite respect and surrounded with carefully guarded secrecy. His household consists of numerous wives, pages, guards and advisors. Around the turn of the century, the Fon of Kom had hundreds of wives, and he had more than a hundred when the British took control of Cameroon. The numerous wives and children at the palace served to enhance the Fon's prestige and demonstrate his wealth, in addition to consolidating alliances with other kingdoms by intermarriage. Royal wives functioned primarily as the Fon's farmers and cooks, and were recruited from among the freeborn population at large. The Fon's extensive rights to claim women in marriage or to dispose of them to others was one of his most important prerogatives and became a source of considerable political struggle in the colonial era. Important roles at the palace were fulfilled by a variety of pages, retainers and messengers.

Another important role in the Fon's household is reserved for the "queen-mother", the so-called Nafoyn, usually the most senior woman of the Fon's matrilineage; the Nafoyn was without a doubt the most influential woman in the kingdom. Though she did not have institutionalized political or judicial powers, she was in a position to advise the Fon personally on a wide range of matters. Fon Yu died in 1912.

During his reign, Kom had prospered economically, power had been centralized, consolidated and enhanced by colonial support, and the territorial boundaries of the kingdom had been expanded. Laikom had increased in population and in ritual importance, numbering more than 250 houses and over 1000 inhabitants in 1912. As a result of increasing population pressure at Laikom and controversies among some royal lineages, several new settlements had been founded a short distance away from the Laikom, including Njinikom and Fanantui[14] .After his death in 1912, Fon Yu was succeeded by Fon Ngam, at the close of German rule in Cameroon. Ngam's dealings with the German administration reveal some of the incipient conflicts troubling the Kom kingdom around the turn of the century. Prior to his succession to the throne, Ngam, then heir apparent, had presumably made himself unpopular: his inauguration was a troubled one, as he was embroiled in a conflict with three other princes of the blood, and several of Yu's sons[15]

Though there are conflicting accounts as to the nature of the quarrel, it appears these royals refused to recognize Ngam as Fon, perhaps because He abolished the practice, which permitted senior princes of the blood to marry the widows of the deceased Fon. Fearing opposition to his rule, Ngam accused these princes of treason. The German authorities had the new Fon's opponents executed, upon which some of Yu's widows committed suicide. Fon Ngam was cursed, such that future chiefs were allegedly robbed of their power of protective clairvoyance[16] The Nafoyn at that time, Naya'a, went into voluntary exile, taking a contingent of followers with her, to demonstrate her disapproval of Ngam's methods, refusing to live at Laikom after she returned to Kom many years later. Ngam's royal rivals, including the Nafoyn, became Christians and moved away from the palace[17]. Naya'a was the first highly placed royal to convert to Christianity. Though the intricacies and implications of this episode are not clear, it is evident that Fon Ngam's position as omnipotent ruler was disputed, at least by some royals, from the early days of his reign. It is also clear that marriage politics were a volatile source of conflict, and that Fon Ngam was not averse to collaborating with the German rulers to enhance his own power.

GERMAN COLONISATION AND CHRISTIANITY

From 1884 until the defeat of Germany in the First World War, Cameroon was officially a German protectorate, Kamerun[18]. German rule met with fierce resistance: when the First World War broke out in 1914, German authority had yet to be established in large parts of the territory. All forms of passive and armed resistance imaginable plagued the German administration throughout its presence in Cameroon. The Bamenda Grassfields provided the German colonizers with heavy, armed resistance. From 1888 until 1912, German rule in the Grassfields was characterized by brutal military expeditions. Large parts of the Grassfields were brought under German rule as late as 1907.

Germany's aim in colonizing Cameroon was above all an economic one. Unlike her successors, Britain and France, who were at least nominally subject to conditions stipulated by the League of Nations, Germany had no philanthropic motives whatsoever in the colonizing enterprise, nor did she so much as attempt to disguise her economic interests in terms of a civilizing mission. This purely economic aim inevitably had repercussions on the form of government and the relationship with indigenes. The German presence in Cameroon ended due to the outbreak of the First World War, which prompted Britain and France to invade the territory. The greatly outnumbered German forces were forced to retreat from Cameroon in December 1915, when Colonel Zimmerman fled to Spanish Guinea with most of the German troops[19]. The ensuing internment of the German troops and their supporters on the island of Fernando Po constitutes an important episode in Cameroonian colonial history: by German estimates, almost 15,000 people made the exodus from Cameroon, slightly less than 1000 of them Europeans [20]

The policy adopted by German colonial authorities with regard to missions may be termed pragmatic. Missionaries were welcome to the protectorate as long as they contributed to the colonial effort, for example, by providing education in the German language. The lack of government initiative resulted in a near-monopoly on education by missionary organizations. The first missionary organization to concern itself with Cameroon was the English Baptist Mission, which was taken over in 1886 by the Protestant Basel Mission, as the Baptists had encountered difficulties with the

German colonial authorities[21] Initially, the Basel Mission was considered by the German colonial administration to be more or less a state Church, hence Catholic missions found it difficult to obtain entry to Cameroon[22] In 1889, the Catholic Pallotine Fathers obtained permission to operate in areas not yet covered by the Basel Mission, and established a mission station at Bojongo, near the coast. It appears that the German administrators welcomed the establishment of a Catholic Mission at that time because the Basel Mission had failed to provide German-speaking native clerks and agents. The Basel Mission had also encountered problems with the German government because the mission resisted the colonial government's oppressive measures with regard to forced labour and land expropriation [23]

The Pallotine Fathers identified themselves closely with German colonial policy, using German as the teaching medium and supporting policies of enforced labour.[24] Until the turn of the century, missionary activity was concentrated along the coast, in the area where plantations had been established. In 1903, the Basel Mission opened a mission station in the Bamenda Grassfields, at Bali, but it was not until 1913 that missionaries approached the Kom area. At that point, the Catholic Fathers of the Sacred Heart of Jesus founded a mission station at Fujua, a short distance away from Laikom, the capital of Kom and the palace of the Fon. The same missionaries had established a mission station in 1912 at Nso to the east of Kom, having been sent there by the German government to "mollify the natives" [25]

The German missions relied heavily on the support of local catechists. Most of the early Christians in the Bamenda Grassfields were plantation labourers who had been baptized by the Pallotine Fathers after receiving rigorous religious instruction for two to three years. These catechists taught in schools, prepared catechumens for baptism, explained the catechism and bible stories in so-called doctrine classes, and led the congregation in prayers. In practice, they ran the whole mission during the absence of ordained priests[26]. The outbreak of World War I did not put an end to the German missionary influence in Kom, for the German Schutztruppe in the Bamenda area included three Catholic priests and five brothers[27] In the long run, the influence of these priests was to be far greater than the influence exerted by the pioneer missionaries who had settled at Fujua. Only in 1919 were the Cameroonian soldiers who had been interned in Fernando Po repatriated. In northern Cameroon, German troops maintained control until Garoua was captured by Allied forces in June 1915. As early as September 1914, however, when the Germans had been ousted from Douala, colonial rule in the Bamenda Grassfields had essentially become a British affair. Eventually, the Treaty of Versailles stipulated that Germany should relinquish all her colonies to the Allied and Associated powers, and German Kamerun was divided between Britain and France. This arrangement was ratified in 1922 by the League of Nations.

EVANGELISATION UNDER THE BRITISH

Although British rule was not yet official, the English concerned themselves with missionary activities in Kom as early as 1916, when the D.O. in Bamenda attempted to convince the Roman Catholic Mission to set up a school where former teachers would be taught English. This move may be considered an anomaly, however, for as the war drew to a close the British policy regarding the re-establishment of the missions in the Bamenda Grassfields was far more hesitant. During the unsettled first years of Britain's presence in Cameroon, her attitude towards the missions was marked by suspicion and impatience. The initial investigations of the British colonial authorities had revealed that the Fons and other traditional leaders in the Bamenda Grassfields were, overall, not too enthusiastic about the representatives of the new religion, be they European or Cameroonian. What had begun as an enticing flirt with "white man's" education had evolved into a potential threat to the omnipotence of the previously unchallenged Fons.

Many of them felt threatened by the new religion, and seized the opportunity presented by the change to British rule to pressure the new authorities to limit missionary activities in their territories. The traditional rulers made astute use of the uncertainty accompanying the switch from German to British rule to try to prevent a new wave of missionary activity from undermining their authority. Furthermore, the fact that the Catholic missionaries had been German gave rise to considerable suspicion on the part of the British administration. In post-World War I colonial logic, Catholicism was easily equated with allegiance to Germany.

They interpreted the fact that such a large contingent of Christians from Kom had enlisted in the German army as an indication of the potentially subversive nature of Catholicism, and was quick to associate mission activities with pro-German propaganda. Clearly, the early Christians were perceived to be hazardous not only to the authority of the new colonial government, but also to the authority of the local chiefs. The implied threat to their own authority was not lost on the early British officials.

Thus the fears of the early British administrators went hand in hand with the interests of traditional rulers, on whose support the British depended heavily. Though they may have overestimated the direct subversive potential of the young Christian Church, the British fears were not entirely unfounded. The German Missionaries and the Agents at Fernando Po were in constant communication with natives in this Division. In one of the letters written during the transitional periods, the fear of these Christians was seen to be much alive. The colonial officer went on to say: If the missions are re- opened before a definite conclusion in the war is arrived at and before we know whether this portion of the Cameroons is to be British Territory or not I cannot help thinking that an altogether erroneous impression will be formed by the native mind. Clearly, the new colonial administration found itself in a precarious dilemma.[28]

The situation, which the British inherited from the Germans, included a Christianized population and the beginnings of westernized elite. By keeping the missions out of Cameroon, the British would be certain to alienate that part of the African population, while at the same time signing the death warrant for the many schools, which had been started by the various missions. Allowing the missions to continue their activities uncontrolled, however, would most certainly alienate a significant other part of the population, including the so-called natural rulers on whose loyalty the British so much relied. Not only foreign missionaries posed a threat to English rule, so did independent Africans. Besides, the influence of missions had in the past proved singularly difficult to assess.

The chiefs in the Bamenda area believed that the autonomy of the Christian "boys" undermined their traditional authority Suffice it to say here that in the first years of British rule, colonial mission policy was critical and cautious. From the very beginning, the colonial administration found itself entangled in a power struggle between Christian converts and tradition, which was to continue throughout the ensuing decades, repeatedly posing an indirect but keenly felt threat to British hegemony.

Regarding Christian missions, both Germany and Britain were guided by pragmatic motives, and both co-operated with the missions to a certain degree in order to further their own aims: economic exploitation, the supply of labour, and the "socialization" of the natives along colonial lines. The result was, initially, ad hoc and sometimes contradictory policy, informed by the colonial government's dilemma: wanting on the one hand to preserve and strengthen traditional authority, and on the other hand striving to allow for "modernizing" influences in the form of Christianity and education.

THE SACRED HEART MISSIONARIES IN KOM

In 1903, when the Basel Mission opened a mission station in the Bamenda Grassfields, at Bali, and in 1913 the Catholic Fathers of the Sacred Heart of Jesus founded a mission station at Fujua, a short distance away from Laikom, a Catholic priest and two brothers were granted land at Fujua to build a station and establish a school, with a three-year educational programme entirely in German.[29] In 1913, the school boasted an enrolment of 120 boys, of whom seven were sons of Fon Ngam.[30] The German mission station was far from completed when the missionaries were forced to leave the area late in 1915. It is difficult to determine how these early missionaries were received in Kom. Most informants maintain that, originally, Fon Ngam had been apprehensive, but not hostile, towards the missionaries, having given them one of his own pipes to indicate his goodwill. According to Nkwi, Fon Ngam warmly received them and gave them a rich fertile area at Fujua[31]. He further maintains, "The Fon was very keen on their work especially the school." The apparently harmonious relationship between the Fon and the missionaries is further indicated by the fact that, when the German missionaries were banned from Kom, they brought all their valuables and books to the Fon for safekeeping during their absence, clearly intending to continue after the war where they had been forced to leave off. All whites were regarded with a certain degree of suspicion because of the Fon's previous encounters with German soldiers. It seems plausible that the mission was allocated land very close to the Fon's palace in order that the Fon might be in a position to keep a close eye on the activities of the missionaries. Oral testimonies suggest that Ngam's interest in the mission stemmed primarily from the advantage he imagined Kom people would gain by taking part in "white man's" education. Whatever the case the Fon's allegiance to the German Catholics was motivated not by a genuine acceptance of the new religion, but by curiosity and the advantage his fondom might gain by co-operating with the priests than by resisting them overtly. The Fon might have been left with little options available taking into account the fact that German colonial government's big stick remained a threat in the face of any blatant refusal of the request of the missionary.

The ostensibly friendly reception granted the missionaries by the Fon did not imply that the people of Kom were prepared to demonstrate the same tolerance towards the new religion. Some Cameroonians were pleasantly surprised that the German missionaries "were not like the German soldiers whom they had met so often, but early British reports refer to a history of tense relations between the Kom converts and the non-Christian population. Non-Christians appeared to be particularly annoyed by the alleged seduction of their women by Christian men[32].

Following the defeat of the Germans in Cameroon, the French and British Governments rushed to apportion the spoils of war. The British like the French could not tolerate in their own backyard the presence of missionaries whose nationality was not of their own. To fill the Vacuum the colonial office in London requested the British Missionaries to take over the German missions. In November 1921 Rev., John Campling a Scottish Priest was assigned to lead the first group of Mill Hill Missionaries to Cameroon. On Sunday, march 26, 1922 the first band of the Mill Hill Missionaries landed ashore at Victoria.

AFRICAN CHRISITANITY IN RETROSPECT

The epoch of missionary endeavours in Africa on a large scale was also the age of great scientific inventions. The discoveries in genetics and radiochemistry boosted the optimism and faith in progress that characterised this period. Max Planck laid the foundation for modern physics in 1900, with research in Quantum physics, Bohr became the prime mover in solving the mystery of the structure of the atom, Friedrich Nietzsche, Sigmund Freud, Carl Jung, and Charles Darwin helped shape the current thought patterns. However, many of the missionaries who came to Africa were without the benefit of the knowledge of African anthropology, Religion and Philosophy and with at best very vague and misconstrued ideas of African customs and traditions. They thus plunged themselves into a very strange and unfamiliar terrain. The Missionaries who began this modern phase of Christian expansion in Africa were devout, sincere, and dedicated men but they were not necessarily theologians. They were more concerned with practical evangelisation, education, and healthcare than with any academic or theological issues that arose from the presence of Christianity in Africa.[33]

Spurred on by the missionary theology of the time and zeal for the salvation of souls, the early missionaries went into action even at the risk of their own lives. Tropical disease infested equatorial rain forest unfamiliar and dangerous terrain, which claimed the lives of many literally cropping them in the vigour of their youth, were not enough to deter, scare, or even enfeeble their spirits. Writing about the Nigerian Mission, Forestal goes on to say: It was a pattern that was to repeat itself with sad regularity during the years that followed. New missionaries continued to arrive from Europe and were carried off by malaria, dysentery, sleeping sickness, yellow fever or some other ailment within months of their arrival. It was to be the pattern of the early years of the Nigerian mission which were years of immense sacrifice and bitter failure. Nigeria lived up to its reputation as 'the white man's grave' and the mortality rate among the missionaries was very high.[34] During the twenty-four years of evangelization in Cameroon, the Pallotine Fathers had lost nine priests, twenty-two brothers, and five sisters.[35]

COLONIAL AND MISSIONARY MOTIVES

Missionaries over the centuries naturally have followed their colonial powers. It was also natural that Christianity and colonisation were introduced into the country at the same time. The fact that Christianity in Cameroon came in the wake of colonisation has made it almost impossible for many people to dissociate Christianity from the trappings of western culture. They perceive Christianity as part of the package offered by the colonial powers. Colonial accounts leave no one in doubt that the colonial powers had no other motive than economic. German colonial accounts in Cameroon put it bluntly: "If new resources are not created, and if one does not work along the lines of the old school, as seen above, the exclusive exploitation of all these products, taking into a account only the good instantaneous finances of the colony, will continue to work and not be able to say nothing other than wastage created and sustained by the state which will not in the future prevent the consequences except with extraordinary means. A farsighted colonial economy should pay its attention for now on the unexploited resources; these are the land and soil; the natives living on these must be exhorted to discover the treasures, which are found beneath the soil. The future of Africa is in the cultivation of plantations by the natives under state control. Plantation economy has begun and European capital has been pulled into Cameroon, now the question is; if this capital will produce profit? As long as there is a probability, everything should be done to favour and sustain the cultivation of plantations while waiting that these produce the promising sources of revenues for the years to come. The Plantation economy as practised by the Europeans only produces profits milieu. The natives had to consecrate or be constrained to engage in the plantation economy. .If one does it through a friendly proposal no black will do it. By imposing it on them, no one of good conscience will agree[36].

Although the main motive of colonial enterprise were economic, certain derivatives of this enterprise bordered on humanism. Whether these were externalities or spilled-over, western colonial authorities found certain prevailing practices abhorrent, detestable and naturally thought it incumbent on them to put an end to these practices. Human sacrifice, reckless and ruthless tribal war fare, ordeals were gradually brought to a halt by these western powers.

Powerful monarchs, almost an enigma in some places were gradually demobilised and dispossessed by keeping a tight rein on them. One of these Monarchs whose authority was eroded beyond expectation and almost became a prisoner in own Fondom was the Fon of Kom. In 1924, D.O. Hunt commented on the intransigence of the Fon, "His trouble is of long standing, and likely to be perennial, until the new social order regarding the foretime sacrosanct wives of a chief is accepted, as it will have to be accepted. (...) The Chief is cutting himself off from some 2000 of his people because twenty-five of his numerous wives have left him.[37] The new social and political order had indeed reduced the Fon almost to a ceremonial head. The most humiliating act was when he was taken from his palace to Njinikom to reopen the church he had closed.

Economic motives remained foreign to the missionaries whose sole preoccupation was the worth and salvation of human souls. In 1919, the pope went on to lament on what he saw as the scandalous and disheartening behaviour of some missionaries who had begun to imitate the greed of the colonialist. "We have been deeply saddened by some recent accounts of missionary life, accounts that displayed more zeal for the profit of some particular nation than for the growth of the kingdom of God. We have been astonished at the indifference of their authors to the amount of hostility these works stir up in the minds of unbelievers. This is not the way of the Catholic missionary, not if he is worthy of the name. No, the true missionary is always aware that he is not working as an agent of his country, but as an ambassador of Christ. And his conduct is such that it is perfectly obvious to anyone watching him that he represents a Faith that is alien to no nation on earth, since it embraces all men who worship God in spirit and in truth, a Faith in which "there is no Gentile, no Jew, no circumcised, no uncircumcised, no barbarian, no Scythian, no slave, no free man, but Christ is everything in each of us" (Colossians 3:12). There is another failing that the missionary must scrupulously avoid, and that is the desire to make any profit beyond the acquisition of souls. There is, of course, no need to delay on this point. If a man is the victim of a craving for financial gain, how can he fulfil his obligations of working single-mindedly for the glory of God? Moreover, how can he, for the increase of God's glory, hold himself ready to sacrifice everything he has, even his life, to the work of calling other men back to a state of spiritual health? There is also the fact that this weakness would cost him a great part of his influence with unbelievers - a fact especially cogent if his craving should descend, as it tends to do, to the level of avarice. For as men judge things, this is the meanest of vices. Nothing is more unworthy of the kingdom of God. In this matter then, the truly apostolic man will again follow the advice of the Apostle of the Gentiles, who in a well-known passage wrote to Timothy: "Let us be content if we have food and clothing" (I Timothy 6:8). He will remember too, that St. Paul set such great store by self-denial that, despite the demands of his arduous ministry, he used to provide for his own needs by manual labour.[38]

CATHOLICISM AND AFRICAN TRADITIONAL RELIGION

With this in mind, they set themselves about with the task of rooting out practices, which correctly or erroneously were perceived to be at odds with Christianity; witchcraft, ancestral cult, village deities, polygamy, necromancy remain the object of their missionary efforts and labours. What the missionaries set out to uproot and dismantle was for the Africans, the adherents to be, their natural heritage, the tenets of their religion. These same traditions which became the source of animosity and deep seated suspicion between the African Christians on one hand and the missionaries on the other hand, contained time honoured answers and solutions to many if not all of African life problems. It is because of this reason that many viewed Christianity with deep-seated suspicion and thus distrusted from the very beginning its message and practices. Already early converts to Christianity had an air of superiority over their relatives and tended to pride themselves around disregarding much of the local authorities where it was possible. It is evident from reviews and appeals against decisions of the Native Court that the local native, already a self-willed and stubborn type, becomes even more so after embracing the Roman Catholic faith, and appears to be under the impression that he can totally ignore all native law and particularly that relating to inheritance and ownership of land[39].

In kom, for example where the issue reached alarming proportions, the missionaries alongside early converts remained a thorn in the flesh of traditional rulers seizing every available opportunity to get on the nerves of their traditional leaders. Matters were even made worse when some of the wives took refuge in the mission. The missionaries seldom saw any value in local culture and native institutions.[40] In the face of what the Fon of kom saw as a blatant violation of customary practice, the Fon was forced to petition the colonial Government. The Catholic mission in Njinikom was at the centre of this petition. He went on to demand that "the Roman Catholic mission now controlled by the European aliens who do not understand native customs in our country be removed and replaced by English Missionaries who can make themselves understood by us... they offer insults to my religion, my police and messengers and are continually seducing the wives of my people and even my own women. In order to avoid insults, I have been forced to drive the main road in order to avoid the village, where against orders and wishes they have established a separate community, which refuses to recognize me. The German missionaries were established in site allotted to them by the government, no trouble occurred, and I was glad to have them. The present missionaries refused to occupy the site. I cannot govern my country if missionary intrigue undermines my power"[41] In 1949, the Fon of Kom was confronted by a Mass exodus of royal wives from the palace. A precedent had been set in this regard in earlier years and was closely connected to the missionary presence at Njinikom. The Mass exodus of wives in 1949 was prompted by the visiting mission of the United Nations Trusteeship Council and (reluctant) interventions by the colonial administration. Trouble at the palace began to brew after an article describing the Fon's marital habits, written by a nun at Nso, was published in a missionary periodical in the late 1940s. The article was in fact largely a figment of the nun's imagination, but contained enough truth to resemble the situation at Laikom, and infuriated the Fon who complained that his marital affairs were of no concern to outsiders.

The example that had been set during Fon Ngam's reign by runaway wives was followed on a large scale after his death, by both royal wives and the wives of commoners. Soon after the establishment of the Kom Native Court, the Native Authority declared that all runaway wives living at the mission compound would be served a civil summons unless they returned to their Father's compound until they were able to find the Christian husbands who would refund the bride price previously paid for them. Nafoin, Naya'a Funkuen, who had been exiled from Laikom due to a conflict with Fon Ngam, had become a Christian during her exile. As she was the most influential woman in Kom, Nafoin Naya'a's conversion though controversial, proved to be a great inspiration to many women at the palace

Some Missionaries viewed African Traditional Religion with deep-seated revulsion. Whether it was out of personal weakness of character, ignorance or over zealousness, we cannot say but in 1929, Father Scully allegedly caused a scandal by kicking a native sacrifice. His behaviour provoked critical commentaries from the entire colonial hierarchy, up to the level of the Lieutenant Governor and was considered grave enough to warrant his imprisonment[42] By 1931, mission-state relations had deteriorated to the point that Bishop Rogan was presented with an ultimatum: either the Church would profess her support to the British efforts to strengthen the recognized Native Authorities, or the Catholic mission would be forced to leave the country. Having been left little choice in the matter, Bishop Rogan complied with the government's request, issuing the following statement: In view of the fact that the reprehensible actions of several Mill Hill Fathers have led (the government) to believe that we refuse to recognize the authority (...) of the native Chiefs (I offer) my guarantee that any Father who recklessly interferes in any way with the legitimate business of native Courts and with the lawful jurisdiction of Native Chiefs, will be sent out of the country by me immediately[43]. In fact the Mill Hill mission as a whole was opposed to the British system of Indirect Rule, regardless of the nationality of the priests concerned, because Indirect Rule was largely based on the authority of chiefs, who invariably had large, polygamous households.[44]

PHILOSOPHICAL AND CULTURAL CONSEQUENCES OF CONVERSION TO CHRISTIANITY

To preach Christianity in its totality and expect Africans to adhere to it without reserve was asking the African adherents to exchange one set of customs, beliefs and practices for another set of customs, beliefs and practices. These sets of practices, customs, and beliefs touched on the fundamental concept of African identity, religion, and philosophy of life. Whether Christian missionary work in Africa was to fail or succeed depended very much on how Christianity was presented by the missionaries and how it was perceived and received by the African convert and their own relatives. The real test of Christianity as in every age naturally presented itself during the very unset of Christianity. The perennial question, which remains very relevant to our time, whether one, could be a true Christian and a true African at the same time. Missionary Christianity was not from the start, prepared to face a serious encounter with either the traditional religions and philosophy or modern changes taking place in Africa.[45]

Literal and historical accounts present us with evidence of many adherents to Christianity who had to come to terms with what it meant to embrace Christianity. Notables who became Christians were rewarded for their allegiance to Christianity by their tribesmen with cultural isolation, stripped of their titles, persecuted, or simply ostracised. Christianity no doubt, was a threat to the foundations of ethnic groups, alongside their creed and customs, which had stood the test of time. These were the very values Africans converting to Christianity had to abandon. In the Bamenda highlands, one of these notables who paid the full price was Pa Martin Atang, founder and first catechist of Mankon. "Happy with his new found Religion, they were anxious, to return home and introduce it to their people...but the village chief and his notables did not welcome their religion. Instead, they became very hostile to Martin, ostracised him and did not want to see him in the village. He was further stripped off his title, Tabara – a title he had held before leaving Bamenda hill top station in search of work with the Whiteman. This title ranks him first among the nobles of the clan, the kingmakers. He was given the nickname 'Tizibong' which means 'one who does not know the good.'[46] The scenario in Bafmeng was of a different magnitude, involving Christians and not simply and individual. The Christians began to criticise the pagans for their polygamy and their sacrifices. The pagans became angry. In some cases, they tore away the medals from the women's necks, ground them, and put them into water for the women to drink. They beat the catechumens who went to doctrine. The chief finally drew a line in old town between the "pagan town" and the "mission." No juju would humbug the Christians as long as they stayed on their own side of the line[47]. In Nso the Fon, obviously, was not prepared to brook such an open and ominous challenge to this retrieved authority: arrests, scourgings, lockings up became the daily lot of the Christians...if the interregnum between the German expulsion and the setting up of the Franco-English condominium had lasted long, blood would have been shed and some would have died for Christ among the Nso clansmen.[48]

Wherever the African is, there is his religion, he carries it to the fields where he is sowing seeds or harvesting a new crop, he takes it with him to the beer party or to attend a funeral ceremony: and If he is educated he takes religion with him to the examination room at the school or the university, if he is a politician he takes it to the house of parliament...To be human is to belong to the whole society, and to do so involves participating in the beliefs, ceremonies, rituals and festivities of that community. A person cannot detach himself from the religion of his group, for to do so is to be severed from his roots, his foundations, his context of security, his kinship and the entire group of those who make him aware of his existence... therefore to be without religion amounts to self-excommunication from the entire life of the society and African people do not know how to exist without religion.[49] This was the reason why Christianity from its humble beginnings in Africa as a whole was seen as a danger to tribal foundations and those who ventured to embrace and flirt with the Whiteman's religion might not have fully understood what they were embracing. The fate of these early adherents to Christianity was swift and total. They were forced to move into Christian villages or enclaves or face ostracisation. Converts relinquished to a large degree their position within traditional society. The price they paid for the perceived benefit of Christianity often amounted to ostracisation. Former networks providing social and emotional security frequently ceased to function as such when someone chose to affiliate with the new religion. The dependence of the converts on the Church community was, by consequence, far reaching.[50]

Largely the work of evangelisation remained a daunting task with seemingly insurmountable obstacles. Without the benefit of language, anthropological knowledge and other aids to evangelisation it seemed almost impossible to communicate so deep a mystery to one by another whose language was foreign. The African mindset and worldview were fundamentally very different from the western mindset of the missionary. Coupled with these were concrete African beliefs, which were at odds with Christianity and therefore mutually exclusive with fundamental Christian beliefs. It is partly for this reason that some people have wondered whether a true and complete conversion to Christianity is possible. Christianity made no positive attempt to incorporate ancestors and witches, song and dance into the Christian scheme[51] This was not always the case, For example, in the Ibo land in Nigeria, Shanahan was to find out that Ekwenze was a formidable enemy, that jujus had strange and unaccounted powers of evil, that bad bush was not given its name without good reason. The longer he stayed in Africa, the more conscious he was to become of Satan as a living active force opposed to the work of the missionary[52] To counter the influence of Ekwenze the missionaries dedicated their new mission to St. Michael the archangel, conqueror of the forces of Satan. A large statue showing the saint crushing the demon was brought in from Europe.

The African continent has Christians who belong to the first, second, third and even fourth generation of Christians. Naturally, new values are easily imbibed more successfully over successive generations. One of the questions, which have not eluded the attention, and interest of missiologists is the question of motives underlying Mass conversions of Africans to Christianity. Nevertheless, full conversion is never a point in history: it is always a process affecting the inner man and his total environment. It may take several generations to reach maturity in a given community. But even then it requires a continual renewal if the conversion is to become relevant at every given moment in history.[53]

EVANGELISATION AND CONVERSION MODELS

Conversion models and circumstances in African societies seem radically different from what was obtained in the western world. Whereas in Europe religion followed the crown in Africa, the crown in many place posed an obstacles to religion and conversion of traditional rulers was not commonplace. In many instance the traditional rulers welcome Christianity mainly for the benefit of education and healthcare Christianity could bring. Christianity has expanded rapidly in the first half of this century, through the joint effort of overseas missionaries and African converts. Schools became the nurseries of Christian congregations. The same buildings were used as schools from Monday to Friday and as Churches on Saturday (for the catechumenate) and Sundays (for worship). It is the Africans who have been to school that are most deeply affected by modern changes[54].

Missionaries constantly presented education as a bait. Nowhere was this more evident than in Nigeria. Shanahan introduced a system of widespread contact in which the missionary staked his claim and moved on, leaving intensive instruction and development until later. He also made a firm commitment to education, having decided that it was possible to transform Ibo society by the means of school and to use all the resources of the mission to achieve such a transformation. These decisions laid the foundation for a phenomenal expansion of the Church among the Ibo people which was unparalleled elsewhere in Africa except in Uganda.

The presence of a colonial power was an important factor in this progress. In 1900, the British, after nearly sixty years of trading on the Niger, began to establish a colonial administration in the area. This brought new ideas, new laws, and a new authority, which challenged traditional beliefs and values. The colonial authorities never set out to dismantle the traditional religion but nonetheless contributed to its eclipse. In a bid to establish law and order, the excesses of the powerful secret societies themselves considerably weakened. In 1901, government forces destroyed the organization of the Long juju because it had become a slave-trading ring. Gradually, traditional religion was robbed of much of its power and a void was created which Christianity was poised to fill. Initially, it was education, which offered an entry point for the missionary. The Ibos developed an insatiable thirst for education, which was seen as the way forward for the tribe in the new dispensation. Education opened the door to the employment opportunities offered by the colonial administration and became the focus of intense competition among rival clans and villages.

Every village wanted a school and was prepared to pay for it. The government, too, was keen to develop an educational programme and, in 1903 offered to assist education by means of grants and professional supervision. The Churches, as voluntary agencies involved in education, were eligible for these grants on condition that they guaranteed that religion would be optional subject on the curriculum. The Anglican Church Missionary Society refused to accept this condition and had to forgo government aid for a time. Joseph Shanahan agreed to the condition, having judged rightly that the vast majority of parents would have no objection to their children being instructed in the white man's religion. He cooperated fully with the government and sat on a Commission for Education, which was established in 1906.

He accomplished his objective by stationing priests in a few strategic points where they would open a school and then use the best students of their school as temporary teachers for subsidiary bush schools in the surrounding areas. After a time these apprentices were replaced by other students. They would then return to finish their own training, whereupon they would go out to open new schools from which the snowballing process could continue in geometric progression. After a few years of this procedure, the original mission became the vibrant centre of an enthusiastic Christian generation.

The school finally broke down the barriers that had stood for so long between the missionaries and the Ibo people. Joseph Shanahan wrote in 1912, in a letter to Rome. "So far we cannot but congratulate ourselves on the fidelity of children, and on the goodwill of the pagans. The school keeps the missionary in contact with the people, because the children give him free entry into every house. He is no longer a stranger but a member of the family. This fact alone makes what he can affect, and what he can prevent, incalculable. He is known everywhere, and he alone can go through the country without danger. Other Europeans dare not move about the country unescorted. But at the very moment of writing, our presence is being demanded in some fifty towns."[55]

CHRISTIAN VILLAGES AND EARLY CONVERTS TO CHRISTIANITY

Evangelization models inevitably leads to a specific pattern of Christian thought, behaviour, and ecclesial communities in response to specific models of evangelisation. A classical case was the work of the Holy Ghost Missionary in eastern Nigeria. The French missionaries fancied the concept of Christian villages in Africa. These villages were intended to be settlements where new converts could live a full Christian life without interference from their pagan neighbours and build up a Christian presence in the country. In Nigeria, these villages had become places where the outcasts of the society were taking refuge. These were former slaves, some of them runaways, others bought by the mission funds collected in Europe, there were abandoned children and orphans, there were cripples, and lepers and homeless old people, there were criminals and murderers, there were also those who for one reason or the other could not fit into the traditional tribal pattern.[56] The early converts could as well rejoice at Paul's words to the Corinthians. Brothers, think of what you were when you were called. Not many of you were wise by human standards; not many were influential; not many were of noble birth. However, God chose the foolish things of the world to shame the wise; God chose the weak things of the world to shame the strong. He chose the lowly things of this world and the despised things—and the things that are not—to nullify the things that are, so that no one may boast before him. It is because of him that you are in Christ Jesus, who has become for us wisdom from God—that is, our righteousness, holiness and redemption. Therefore, as it is written: "Let him who boasts boast in the Lord.[57] Commenting on this passage Pope Benedict XVI went on to say, "We must add a further point of view. The *First Letter to the Corinthians* (1:18-31) tells us that many of the early Christians belonged to the lower social strata, and precisely for this reason were open to the experience of new hope, as we saw in the example of Bakhita. Yet from the beginning, there were also conversions in the aristocratic and cultured circles.[58] The philosophy of the early missionary endeavour seems to have been that to build a Christian edifice sure, secure, and solid; you had to create a cultural void. To men so dedicated, who braved the wild unknown to plant the cross and spread the word, it appeared a priori dangerous to concede that there was in African culture any thing on which a genuine Christianity could be built. Their ardent zeal, their candid favour led them instinctively to dump the whole lot of it as totally pernicious. If you made one concession, however innocent, you did not know where it would end. The convert must be voided and washed clean and shorn of the mind he had inherited from heathen ancestors. Today this policy is bitterly inveighed against by the protagonist of African culture. Was this policy right or wrong? That is a pointless quarrel; each policy or philosophy or institution must be judged in the light of the zeitgeist in which it prevailed.[59] In this Christian village, daily Mass and communion, as a matter of course, became the centre of life. There were protracted community payers morning and evening, doctrine classes at dawn and dusk for children and catechumens; and once every week for the young and the grown-ups, weekly confessions and extra religious knowledge classes daily on the school timetable. Thrice everyday the angelus rang out, at break of the day, at noon, and at sundown and every one stood where he was to commemorate the incarnation[60].

The early Christian converts were often regarded with scorn. Achebe in his Novel Things Fall Apart gives us an idea of these early converts. None of his early converts was a man whose words were heeded in the assembly of the people. None of them was a man of title. They were mostly the kind of people that were called efulefu, worthless empty men. The imagery of an efulefu in the language of the clan was a man who sold his machete and wore the sheath to battle. Chielo, the priestess of Agbala, called the converts the excrement of the tribe, and the new faith was a mad dog that had come to eat them up.[61]

Not only were the early Christians regard with scorn and disdain they were often made to be the prey. It is precisely for this reason that the land allocated to them was in the minds of the people spiritually the most dangerous land to inhabit. Achebe offers some more insights into the idea of Bad bush or evil forest. Every clan and village had its own evil forest. In it were buried all those who died of the evil diseases, like leprosy and small pox. It was also the dumping ground for the potent fetishes of great medicine men when they died. An evil forest was therefore, alive with the sinister forces and power of darkness. It was such a forest that the missionaries were usually given to settle. The village elders were not keen on having missionaries in their villages and avoiding them would have been very offensive. They gave the missionaries the forest with the hope that no one in his right frame of mind would accept. It was such a piece of land that was given to the early missionaries. Writing about the evil forest or bad bush as it was called, and the resultant consequences, Forristal, quoting from an Ibo chronicler, writes that the priest had been asked not to touch the bush because it was bad bush, and the haunt of evil spirits. As work went on the children contracted various diseases. Some of them died, some were very sick and others were paralysed. The power of the juju and the fetish is one of perennial unsolved mysteries of African life.[62]

The protestant and Catholic forms of Christianity have meant separating Africans from their society and putting them on the side of the European.[63] It was a system that had so many shortcomings. In Nigeria, a change was soon initiated when it was discovered that Christian villages would lead them nowhere. However if there were to be any meaningful future for the missions a change of strategy was necessary. The missions were no longer to be a refuge for the work-shy and the unwanted. No more motherless babies were to be accepted. ...Lepers, cripples, old women, children would all have to give whatever help they could to support themselves and the mission.[64]

Before this reversal in policy, the work was confined to a few mission stations close to the Niger River, in towns and villages already influenced by British administration and trade. The early adherents were, for the most part, former slaves who had been ransomed by the missionaries or liberated by the British authorities. These were grouped together in villages where it was hoped they would live the Christian life and become bearers of Christianity to the surrounding countryside. The custom of grouping people in villages under the authority of the missionary existed in South America in the early sixteenth century and was used to great effect by Jesuit missionaries, especially in Paraguay, in the seventeenth and eighteenth centuries. In nineteenth century Africa, the Christian village emerged again in Catholic and Protestant missions.[65]

No sooner had a settlement been effected, than the missionaries began to experience the difficulties of life in a tribal area. The last thing they desired was to create a new separate Africa; yet again and again they found themselves at the centre of a new settlement, made up of freed slave children, of men who for some reason had lost their identity with their tribe, of criminals fleeing from justice (murderers not excluded!) and of young men who wished to learn the skills that only the white man could teach[66]. The early Christian community in Njinikom had certain features, which gradually brought it to resemble a Christian village in some sense. For example writing about the truce, Shortly after enthronement of the Fon of kom, he announced that Churches would be permitted to be opened in three populous Kom quarters, besides Njinikom, for a probationary period of six months, during which the Christians were expected to return to their home villages and to prove themselves amenable to the authority of the chief and the Quarter Heads. By stimulating the establishment of Churches in various locations, Ndi hoped to disperse the Christian community at Njinikom. Most people living at Njinikom came from elsewhere, and it was considered preferable that people moved back to their own villages and families, practising their religion there.[67]

The situation at Esu was in many ways a mini version of the Njinikom scenario. In 1935, a Christian settlement had been established in Esu. About 20 men had settled on mission grounds there with an unknown number of women and children in a compound, containing about 10 buildings.[68] In the nearby Nso fondom, in Shisong which had become a save haven for the new converts, the only effective authority was that of the priest. The Nwerong or kwihfon, the embodiment and executor of the chiefly power, revered and feared throughout Nso country feared being unmasked and beaten if he set foot in Shisong. There was a song in my childhood days: "Shisong she kwenni she nyuy." This Shisong once of the Fon's now is of God.[69] The Sixas though not a Christian village in any sense certainly operated with the same philosophy of Christian villages. In every mission in the southern Cameroon there is building which houses, in principle, all the young girls engaged to be married. This is the Sixa. All our girls who want to marry in the strict Catholic way may stay in the sixa for two to four months, except in exceptional cases, which are always many. The defenders of this institution praise its usefulness, if not its necessity[70].

THE TRIPLE HERITAGE AND SHATTERED DREAMS

Colonization, Christianity and African culture have made it almost impossible for anyone to avoid the consequence of a triple heritage. This has not been without consequences for Christianity. It bears not only the stigma of colonialism, foreignness, westernism and paternalism but also the potentialities and strength of organization, institutionalism, and links with the historical traditions of Christendom, financial resources, personnel from overseas...[71]. In 1931, the colonial government, represented by Resident Arnett, was convinced of the inevitable Christianization of Kom. In the Resident's opinion, the Kwifon, the executive arm of the Fon's government, was destined to disappear because the younger generation was less easily impressed by the secrecy and solemnity traditionally surrounding the Kwifon, and increasingly challenged the religious foundation of the Kwifon: The Christian opposes Kwifon as part of his duty to his new faith. The ex-school pupil feels superior to the mystery and ceremony by which the Kwifon imposes on the credulous multitude. The trader and traveller (...) ridicules the pretensions of Kwifon and resists all authority[72] His estimate was that before long the ruler of the kingdom would himself be a Christian, rendering administration together with the non-Christian Kwifon impossible: It cannot be many years before we find (...) that the proper successor is a Christian and refuses to take any part in the Kwifon or that several of the leading men who ought to have a controlling voice in the chief's public actions are standing outside public affairs because they are Christians and will not take place on a Kwifon Council.[73] The Resident was not far from the truth. Fon Michael Njinabo was a Christian when he became Fon. He was the grand son of the Nafoin Naya'a the first queen mother to become a Christian during the reign of Fon Ngam. Fon Michael Njinabo was not the only Christian who became Fon, Fon Vincent Yuh, who was also among the early princesses who followed Nafoin Naya'a Fukuen into exile was also baptised, succeeded the royal throne.

The number of Catholics in this archdiocese today is 170.081, in a population of one million people. This means that Catholics constitute only 17.31% of the total population of the Archdiocese. Very many of our fellow citizens in this Archdiocese are adherents of African Traditional Religion. On the whole, it can be said that they are open to Christianity. It is our mission to bring the good news to them, and to bring them to the waters of baptism.[74] After almost close to a century of evangelisation it can be rightly said, "Well over 50% of the inhabitants in the territory of the archdiocese of Bamenda is made up of the adherents of African Traditional Religion. In general, they are favourably disposed towards Christianity, probably because of the Church's work in such fields as education and Health Care. It is the impression of the local ordinary that an all out drive to reach the adherents of African Traditional Religion would be richly rewarded in terms of genuine conversions if only the apostolic personnel, especially priests and catechists are available in a measure more adequate than is the case at present. It is hoped that with the present formation programmes organized for catechists in the Archdiocese of Bamenda that impression would begin to become a reality in the not so remote future.[75]

Notes

1. John Paul II Post-Synodal Apostolic Exhortation Ecclesia in Africa on the Church in Africa and its Evangelizing mission towards the year 2000 no.33.

2. NDI, Anthony Mbunwe (1983), Mill Hill Missionaries and the State in Southern Cameroons, 1922-1962, London.

3. CHILVER, Elizabeth M. (1963), 'Native Administration in the West Central Cameroons, 1920-1954.' in K. Robinson & F. Madden (eds.), Essays in Imperial Government, Oxford: 89-139.

4. NKWI, Paul Nchoji (1976), Traditional Government and Social Change. A study of the political institutions among the Kom of the Cameroon Grassfields, Freibourg.

5. Ibid.: 23.

6. CHILVER, Elizabeth M. (1963), 'Native Administration in the West Central Cameroons, 1920-1954.' in K. Robinson & F. Madden (eds.), Essays in Imperial Government, Oxford: 89-139.

7. Nkwi 1976: 140 op.cit.

8. Pius XII, Saeculo Exeunte Octavo, Encyclical letter on the Eighteen Century of the Independence of Portugal no.6.
9. Ibid no.7.
10. WARNIER, Jean-Pierre (1993), 'The King as a Container in the Cameroon Grassfields.' Paideuma. Mitteilungen zur Kulturkunde 39:291-in 302. in De Vries Jacqueline (1998) Catholic Mission, Colonial government and Indigenous Response in Kom (Cameroon) African studies centre.
11. Ibid
12. The words Secular and religious do not mean much to the African. The separation between what is sacred and what is secular does not particularly fit in African Philosophy and Religion.
13. Chilver & Kaberry op.cit.
14. Nkwi op. cit.
15. Chilver & Kaberry 1967: 149 op cit.
16. ibid.
17. Nkwi op.cit.
18. The name Kamerun is used here when referring to the German colonial period.
19. STOECKER, Helmuth (1986), 'Cameroon 1906-1914.' in H. Stoecker (ed.), German Imperialism in Africa: From the Beginnings until the Second World War, London/New York: 161-74. in De Vries Jacqueline (1998) Catholic Mission, Colonial government and Indigenous Response in Kom (Cameroon) African studies centre
20. QUINN, Frederick (1985), 'The Impact of the First World War and its Aftermath on the Beti of Cameroon.' in M.E.P age (ed.), Africa and the First World War, Basingstoke/London: 171-85.
21. NGOH, Victor Julius (1987), Cameroon 1884 - 1985: A Hundred Years of History, Yaoundé.
22. NDI, Anthony Mbunwe (1983), Mill Hill Missionaries and the State in Southern Cameroons, 1922-1962, London.
23. OBDEIJN, H.L.M. (1983), The Political Role of Catholic and Protestant Missions in the Colonial Partition of Black Africa, A Bibliographical Essay, Leiden

24. NDI, Anthony Mbunwe (1986), 'The Second World War in Southern Cameroons and its Impact on Mission-State Relations, 1939-1950.' in D. Killingray & R. Rathbone (eds.), Africa and the Second World War, New York: 204-31. in De Vries Jacqueline (1998) Catholic Mission, Colonial Government and Indigenous Response in Kom (Cameroon) African studies centre.

25. Ibid.

26. Ndi 1986 op.cit.

27. Nkwi 1976 op cit.

28. BNA-Sd 1917/5, DO Podevin to Resident, 8.9.1917 in De Vries Jacqueline (1998) Catholic Mission, Colonial Government and Indigenous Response in Kom (Cameroon) African studies centre.

29. Timneng, Michael, n.d,, autobiography, Njinikom Mission, in De Vries Jacqueline (1998) Catholic Mission, Colonial government and Indigenous Response in Kom (Cameroon) African studies centre.

30. Nkwi 1976 op. cit.

31. Nkwi 1976: op. cit. 158.

32. Nkwi op. cit.

33. MBITI, John (1969), African religions and philosophy, East African Educational Publishers.

34. Desmond Forestal, The Second Burial of Bishop Shanahan. Veritas 1990 p.44.

35. Centenary Album of the **Catholic** Church in Cameroon.

36. Nkwi, Paul Nchoji (1989) German Presence in the **W**estern Grassfields 1891-1913 A German Colonial Account, Leiden.

37. BNA-Cb 1924/3, Annual Report Bamenda Division, 1924, pp.6-7.

38. Benedict XV. Maximum XV (1919) Maximum Illud: Apostolic Letter on the Propagation of the Faith Throughout the world. 30 November 1919. Translated by Thomas J. M. Burke, SJ Washington, DC: National Catholic Welfare Office, no. 20.

39. BNA-Cb 1934/1, Annual Report Bamenda Division, 1935, p.11. in De Vries Jacqueline (1998) Catholic Mission, Colonial Government and Indigenous Response in Kom (Cameroon) African studies centre.

40. Mbunwe in O'Neil in De Vries Jacqueline (1998) Catholic Mission, Colonial government and Indigenous Response in Kom (Cameroon) African studies centre.
41. Petition by the Fon of kom against Roman Catholic Mission to the Divisional Officer of Bamenda Division 1928 in Ndi, Anthony Mbunwe (2004) Mill Hill missionaries in Southern Cameroons, Pauline's publication Africa, Nairobi p330.
42. Ndi 1986: op cit 121.
43. BNA-Sad 1928/2, Mgr. Rogan to Resident, 10.10.1931 in De Vries Jacqueline (1998) Catholic Mission, Colonial government and Indigenous Response in Kom (Cameroon) African studies centre.
44. De Vries Jacqueline ,(1998) Catholic Missions: Colonial Government and Indigenous Response in kom (Cameroon) African Studies Centre.
45. Mbiti, John (1969) African Religions and Philosophy, East African Educational Publishers p.232.
46. Atang, Ade Luke (2000) The struggle for the Catholic priesthood, Macacos.
47. Souvenir, St. Gabriel's Parish Bafmeng silver Jubilee 1965-1990.
48. Fonlon Bernard cited op.
49. Mbiti John S (1967) African Religion and Philosophy. Nairobi, p.2, in Ochiend-Odiambo African Philosophy An Introduction , Consulata Institute of Philosophy.
50. De Vraies, J. op. cit.
51. Mbiti, John (1967) African religion and philosophy East African Educational Publishers Nairobi, 237.
52. Forrestal Desmond,(1990) The Second Burial of Bishop Shanahan, Dublin: Veritas Publications.
53. Mbiti (1967) op. cit.
54. Ibid.
55. Thomas Kiggins (1991) Maynooth Mission to Africa. The story of St. Patrick's Kiltegan. Gill and Macmillan.
56. Forrestal D. Op. cit.
57. 1corinthians 1:26-31.

58. Benedict XVI .Encyclical letter Encyclical letter Spe et Salve on Christian hope no. 5.
59. Fonlon cit op.
60. Fonlon cit op.
61. Achebe Chinua (1981) Things Fall Apart, The New WindMill Series p.130.
62. Cf Forristal (1990) op. cit., p.112.
63. Mbiti, J, op. cit.
64. Ibid.
65. De Vries, J. op. cit.
66. Ibid.
67. Mbiti J, op. cit.
68. De Vries op. cit.
69. Fonlon Benard : A simple story Simply Told (1983) CEPER Yaoundé.
70. Mongo Bet, The Poor Christ of Bomba, Heinemann p.5.
71. De Vries op. cit.
72. BNA-Ia 1926/1, Resident to Secretary of the Southern Provinces, 10.7.1931 in De Vries Jacqueline (1998) Catholic Mission, Colonial Government and Indigenous Response in Kom (Cameroon) African Studies Centre.
73. Ibid.
74. Tatah Mbuy H., Encounter the Truth Jubilee Sermons of Archbishop Paul Verdzekov, Bamenda: Unique Printers pg.17
75. Verdzekov Paul, Quinquinnial Report: Archdiocese of Bamenda: 1999-2004 p.8

CHAPTER TWO

MISSIONARY THEOLOGY

INTRODUCTION
All missionary expeditions in all epochs of human history have been driven by a specific missionary theology. From Pentecost to the missionary endeavours of the fifteenth and nineteenth centuries to the present day, the theological underpinnings of mission have played an important role in either undermining or propelling the missionary fervour. Historical surveys of the different periods of the Church's missionary history attest to this fact. From Pentecost to the edict of Milan, owing to the hostile environment the Church existed almost in the shadows depending on persuasion to win converts to the faith. Once Christianity had reached officialdom, it gradually became incumbent on itself to bring all to the sheepfold. Once the concept of ecclesiasticisation of salvation had taken root there was no turning back on this all out move to enliven the world with the yeast of Christianity. This narrow view of salvation springing from Cyprian and Augustine laid at the root of missionary expeditions from the fourth to the nineteenth century. However with the reformulation, redefinition of these earlier concepts of salvation, flowing from the theological thinking surrounding mission as articulated in the post Vatican II documents, missionary favour suddenly began to wane. It is important to examine how over the centuries the whole concept of salvation has evolved and with what consequences it has had for mission.

APOSTOLIC AND PATRISTIC TIMES
In the first century "Before He returned to His Father, Our Lord Jesus Christ addressed to His disciples the words: "Go into the whole world and preach the gospel to all creation" (Mark 16:15). With these words He committed to them a duty, a momentous and a holy charge, that was not to lapse with the death of the Apostles but would bind their successors, one after another, until the end of the world - as long, that is, as there remained on this earth men whom the truth might set free. Entrusted with this mandate, "they went

forth and preached everywhere" (Mark 16:20) the word of God, so that "through all the earth their voice resounds, and to the ends of the world, their message" (Psalm 18:5). From that time on, as the centuries have passed, the Church has never forgotten that command God gave her, and never yet has she ceased to dispatch to every corner of the world her couriers of the doctrine He entrusted to her, and her ministers of the eternal salvation that was delivered through Christ to the race of men[1]

The Church has never shrunk from its prime responsibility of making it possible for all to come to the sheepfold. In the early Church, the primary concern of Paul was to win as many people for Christ as possible. "I have made myself a slave to all, that I might win the more, to the Jews I became a Jew, in order to win Jews (1Cor 9: 19-23)."He saw humanity as lost on the road to eternal damnation and thus in dire need of salvation. The idea of imminent judgement on those who do not obey the truth (Romans 2: 8) is a recurring theme in Pauline Literature. It was precisely for this reason that Paul allowed himself no relaxation. He saw it as incumbent on him with dire consequence if he failed in this obligation. He had to proclaim this message to as many people as possible. It was a charge laid on him which he saw as an inescapable necessity "Woe to me if I do not preach the gospel" (1Cor 9: 16). Although he saw the preaching of the gospel as a matter of urgency to capture as many people as possible, his main concern was not the wrath of God. His gospel is good news addressed to people who have fully sinned, who are without excuse and who deserve God's judgment. (cf. Romans 1: 20, 23, 2: 5-10) but to whom God in his kindness is providing an opportunity for repentance (Romans 2: 4).The purpose of Paul's mission was above all to lead people to salvation in Christ. In and through his mission, Paul prepares the world for God's coming glory and for the day when all will praise him.[2]

After AD 85 following the fall of Jerusalem and the dispersion of the Jews into the Diaspora, Christianity had to distinguish itself clearly not only from Judaism but also from the Hellenistic religions. Similarly, Christians had to battle on two fronts: against the synagogue and the Hellenistic religions. Christianity had to clearly distinguish itself from any other religion. The common denominator from the apostolic to the patristic times has always been the need to proclaim the gospel. During the patristic period attempts were made to clarify the understanding of mission. The reason and understanding of mission have revolved around the axis of ecclesiastisation of salvation. Once the concept of salvation within the Church had been coined it became incumbent on the Fathers of the Church to make it possible for many people to enter the Church. From Origen to Augustine to Cyprian, the concept of salvation within the Church gradually gained momentum. This concept gradually became the teaching of the Church and the underpinning of missionary movement. One of the early Christian writers whose writings have continued to have an impact on our Christian thought and practice is St. Augustine and Cyprian. Augustine's refutation of Pelagius had a far-reaching impact on medieval concept and theology of mission. Augustine clarified the thoughts of the Church on original Sin and predestination thus affirming the need and necessity of baptism for salvation[3], which could only be administered within the Church.

During the fourth and fifth centuries the Donatists expressed their anger and despair at what they saw as a contrast between the lives of the Church members and office bearers. For them true believer should have nothing to do with the world and with a Church which allowed itself to become contaminated by the world. The true Church must keep itself totally unblemished and perfect; if this does not happen, the sins of the individual members and of office bearers will spread like an infection through the entire Church. They advocated for a total separation between Church and state.

Augustine responded by stating that one who enters the Church...is bound to see drunkards, misers, tricksters, gamblers, adulterers, fornicators, people wearing amulets, assiduous clients of sorcerers, astrologers, the same crowd that presses into the Churches on Christian festivals also fill the theatres on pagan holidays, for in the final analysis the difference between Christians and others lies in one thing only: the former are members of the Church the latter are not.[4] For Augustine authority and holiness were regarded as being part of the institutional Church whether or not the accompanying and expected moral and theological qualities were there or not. Since the worldwide Church founded by the apostles was the only true Church, whoever left it was on the wrong, those who severed their links with this true Church also severed their relationship with the God. Visible unity and salvation went hand in hand; one could not exist without the other. The reason for mission was to make this visible Church to encompass as many people as possible because salvation was found only in the Church and who ever was in the Church was on the road to salvation, whoever was out of the visible Church was on the road to damnation.

During the patristic age, several attempts were made to clarify the concept of the Church and salvation and why mission was important. This understanding of mission and the Church has its roots in Cyprian's famous dictum, extra ecclesiam nulla salus ("there is no salvation outside the Church) a statement of the Patristic period whose misinterpretation was only clarified and reformulated by the Vatican II Council. This statement like the teaching of Augustine on infant baptism born during a stormy period of the controversy with Pelagius over the issue of infant baptism and original sin in the history of the Church was applied universally in the entire Catholic Church. For **Saint Irenaeus** "[The Church] is the entrance to life; all others are thieves and robbers. On this account we are bound to avoid them... We hear it declared of the unbelieving and the blinded of this world that they shall not inherit the world of life which is to come... Resist them in defence of the only true and life giving faith, which the Church has received from the Apostles and imparted to her sons." For **Saint Cyprian** "He who has turned his back on the Church of Christ shall not come to the rewards of Christ; he is an alien, a worldling, an enemy. You cannot have God for your Father if you have not the Church for your mother. Our Lord warns us when He says: 'he that is not with Me is against Me, and he that gathereth not with Me scattereth.' Whosoever breaks the peace and harmony of Christ acts against Christ; whoever gathers elsewhere than in the Church scatters the Church of Christ." For S**aint Augustine** "No man can find salvation except in the Catholic Church. Outside the Catholic Church one can have everything except salvation. One can have honour, one can have the sacraments, one can sing alleluia, one can answer amen, one can have faith in the name of the Father and of the Son and of the Holy Ghost, and preach it too, but never can one find salvation except in the Catholic Church.

MAGISTERIAL TEACHING
13TH CENTURY TO THE 15TH CENTURY

Following the Lateran Council (AD 1215) Pope Innocent III went on to say "One indeed is the universal Church of the faithful, outside which no one at all is saved, in which the priest himself is the sacrifice, Jesus Christ, whose body and blood are truly contained in the sacrament of the altar under the species of bread and wine; the bread (changed) into His body by the divine power of transubstantiation, and the wine into the blood, so that to accomplish the mystery of unity we ourselves receive from His (nature) what He Himself received from ours. Surely no one can accomplish this sacrament except a priest who has been rightly ordained according to the keys of the Church, which Jesus Christ Himself conceded to the Apostles and to their successors. But the sacrament of baptism (which at the invocation of God and the indivisible Trinity, namely, of the Father and of the Son and of the Holy Spirit, is solemnized in water) rightly conferred by anyone in the form of the Church is useful unto salvation for little ones and for adults. In addition, if, after the reception of baptism anyone shall have lapsed into sin, through true penance he can always be restored. Moreover, not only virgins and the continent but also married persons pleasing to God through right faith and good work merit to arrive at a blessed eternity."

The Papal Bull Unam Sanctam of Pope Boniface VII endorsed Cyprian phase quite literally and closed this assertion: "Urged by faith, we are obliged to believe and to maintain that the Church is one, holy, Catholic, and also apostolic. We believe in her firmly and we confess with simplicity that outside of her there is neither salvation nor the remission of sins, as the Spouse in the Canticles [Sgs 6:8] proclaims: 'One is my dove, my perfect one. She is the only one, the chosen of her who bore her,' and she represents one sole mystical body whose Head is Christ and the head of Christ is God [1 Cor 11:3]. In her then is one Lord, one faith, one baptism [Eph 4:5]... "We declare, state, define and proclaim that it is altogether necessary for salvation for every human being creature to be subject to the Roman Pontiff."

The Papal Bull Cantate Domino of Pope Eugene IV, following the Council of Florence (AD 1438-1445) went on to state that "The most Holy Roman Church firmly believes, professes and preaches that none of those existing outside the Catholic Church, not only pagans, but also Jews, heretics and schismatics, can have a share in life eternal; but that they will go into the eternal fire which was prepared for the devil and his angels, unless before death they are joined with Her; and that so important is the unity of this ecclesiastical body that only those remaining within this unity can profit by the sacraments of the Church unto salvation, and they alone can receive an eternal recompense for their fasts, their almsgivings, their other works of Christian piety and the duties of a Christian soldier. No one, let his almsgiving be as great as it may, no one, even if he poured out his blood for the Name of Christ, can be saved, unless he remains within the bosom and the unity of the Catholic Church."

AGE OF EXPLORATION, DISCOVERY AND COLONISATION

Following the discovery of the new world it suddenly became clear that there were millions in the shadow of death and who were certainly on the road to perdition without any means of obtaining salvation. For centuries the Church was convinced that the gospel had reached the ends of the earth. It was on this account that the Pope Benedict XV went on to say "Anyone who studies the facts of this great saga cannot help being profoundly impressed by them: by all the stupendous hardships our missionaries have undergone in extending the Faith, the magnificent devotion they have shown, and the overwhelming examples of intrepid endurance they have afforded us. And to anyone who weighs these facts the realization must come as a shock that right now, there still remain in the world immense multitudes of people who dwell in darkness and in the shadow of death. According to a recent estimate, the number of non-believers in the world approximates one billion souls[5] who were rushing to their perdition on a daily basis.

Even up to 1958 Pope Pius XII, in his encyclical Ad Apostolorum Principis, could rightly say, We teach we declare that the Roman Church by the providence of God hold the primacy of ordinary power over all others and that this is the power of jurisdiction of the Roman Pontiff, which is truly Episcopal and immediate...there is one flock of the Church of Christ under one supreme shepherd. This is the teaching of the Catholic truth from which no one can depart without loss of faith and salvation.[6]

When the missionaries appeared in the horizons of the African continent during the second wave of evangelisation of the nineteenth century, the theology of mission spurring them on was more or less the same. Like the missionary congregation of the time, the theology of mission of the St. Joseph's Society for Foreign Missions was in no doubt perfectly in line with the theology of mission of the time. St. Joseph's Society for Foreign Missions, which carried out most of the work of primary evangelisation of the present day Ecclesiastical Province of Bamenda, was instituted to "Labour for souls that are most abandoned and in the greatest need-that is, for the heathen and unevangelised races." The society's constitution of 1930 went on to state their motives as follows:

A single soul, redeemed by the most Precious Blood, is of greater intrinsic worth than the whole material globe on which we live. In some sense it is worth the infinite price that has been paid for its redemption. Then, one soul admitted into Heaven will render throughout all eternity a greater honour to God than was rendered on Him by the lives of great Saints on earth. The lives of these latter were of short duration, and were attended by some degree of infirmity and sin; whereas the life of a soul in Heaven is eternal and without any, even the slightest, admixture of imperfection. The honour and glory to God arising from the salvation of a single soul, whom we may have conducted to Heaven unspeakable a privilege, therefore, to be invited by God to spend a short life here in labouring for the eternal salvation of souls!

Think of the horrible destruction of souls going on ceaselessly day and night. Their spiritual wreckage covers land and sea. The enemy of God and man is sleepless in his activity and myriads of evil spirits and of human beings are his agents. He never tires, and when defeated begins again. His object is to destroy the work of the Redemption and to fill hell with souls. Regions of the world seem to be his by right of conquest, and he strives to obtain possession of every member of the human race. Think, too, of the most pitiable condition of the heathen world, which, though it has not apostatised from Christianity, lies buried in darkness, bound hand and foot in slavery to Satan. It is awaiting in its deep misery the blessed advent of Christ in the person of the ministers of salvation.

Next, by an inscrutable decree of Providence, even man's eternal salvation is made to depend upon the zeal of his brother man. How few hunger and thirst for God's honour! Explorers and traders think nothing of risking their fortunes and their lives for a little worldly gain and a vain bubble of honour. Men face the severest sufferings and privations to attain some purely human objects. But how few act thus for God, or trust Him to repay in another world their labours to extend His kingdom and to promote His honour and His name in this! It is this want of faith, this worldliness and hardness of heart in Christians that leaves the great Mass of humankind still sitting in the cold region of the shadow of death.

Then let the members of St. Joseph's Society brace themselves to undertake the most arduous labours, by contemplating the lives of Blessed Peter, Prince of the Apostles, and of all the Apostles of Jesus Christ, who, in age after age, have spent their lives and shed their blood for the salvation of souls. Their weary journeying, their continuous teaching, their manifold perils and privations, their bitter sufferings and death are now all over, while they have entered for eternity into the glory and bliss of the Beatific Vision. What they believed, we believe; what they loved, we can love; what they did, what they endured, we, by God's grace, can do and endure. Whither they are gone-into the bosom of the Triune God-we also, by following in their footsteps, can surely go.

Finally, the thought of all that God has done for us individually cannot fail to inspire a generous nature with a desire to co-operate with Him in the work of His special predilection, the salvation of souls. Let a man contemplate all that is generous and loving on the part of God, and personal to himself in the Divine acts of his creation, preservation, and redemption; let him follow, if he can, the wondrous thread of God's graces and mercies to him, running through every day and hour of his existence, and realise how entirely and absolutely dependent he is upon God for everything; let him try to measure how great, how wise, how good and generous and loving God is, both in Himself and towards His children, and he will thirst for opportunities wherein to prove his gratitude, and will say with the Apostle of the Gentiles, Omnia possum in eo qui me confortat.[7]

In 1863, on the 10th of August Pope Pius IX made public his encyclical "Quanto conficiamur moerore, on the Promotion of False Doctrine, among other points the Pope went on to say "Here, too, our beloved sons and venerable brothers, it is again necessary to mention and censure a very grave error entrapping some Catholics who believe that it is possible to arrive at eternal salvation although living in error and alienated from the true faith and Catholic unity. Such belief is certainly opposed to Catholic teaching. Also well known is the Catholic teaching that no one can be saved outside the Catholic Church. Eternal salvation cannot be obtained by those who oppose the authority and statements of the same Church and are stubbornly separated from the unity of the Church and from the successor of Peter, the Roman Pontiff, to whom "the custody of the vineyard has been committed by the Saviour." The words of Christ are clear enough: "If he refuses to listen even to the Church, let him be to you a Gentile and a tax collector;" "He who hears you hears me, and he who rejects you, rejects me, and he who rejects me, rejects him who sent me;" "He who does not believe will be condemned;" "He who does not believe is already condemned;" "He who is not with me is against me, and he who does not gather with me scatters." The Apostle Paul says that such persons are "perverted and self-condemned;" the Prince of the Apostles calls them "false teachers . . . who will secretly bring in destructive heresies, even denying the Master... bringing upon themselves swift destruction."[8]

For centuries the Church had maintained that there is no salvation outside the juridical confines of the early Church. Now it began to admit though in a subtle way that the possibility of salvation outside the Church was a reality. The paradigm shift set in motion by the reformulation of the Church's teaching on ecclesio-centric soteriology which had kept missionary activity buoyant for centuries started at this moment. It was in this document that the supreme pontiff clearly stated that there was a possibility for salvation for those who were often being referred to as the heathen and the unevangelised "There are, of course, those who are struggling with invincible ignorance about our most holy religion. Sincerely observing the natural law and its precepts inscribed by God on all hearts and ready to obey God, they live honest lives and are able to attain eternal life by the efficacious virtue of divine light and grace. Because God knows, searches and clearly understands the minds, hearts, thoughts, and nature of all, his supreme kindness and clemency do not permit anyone at all who is not guilty of deliberate sin to suffer eternal punishments.[9]

For once the wind that had kept the sails of missionary endeavour buoyant began to peter out, to subside and to experience in some place a nosedive. The mandate of the Church to proclaim the gospel was not superseded by the very discovery that one could attain salvation outside the juridical confines of the visible Church. While observing the precarious and volatile situation in Africa with new ideologies following the birth of liberation movements with Marxist leanings, which stood at odds with Christianity, the Church could not but make its voice heard. Most of these movements were not in the best of terms with Christianity and sought to sow seeds of discord in the minds of people in relation to Christianity. In 1957 in his letter, Fidei Donum, on the Conditions of the Catholic Mission, especially in Africa Pope Pius XII went on to say, The gravity of these statements is further increased by the too precipitate course of events - this can be observed everywhere - which has by no means escaped the notice of the Catholic bishops and the leading Catholics. While the peoples of this continent are striving to adopt new ways and new methods (and some of them appear to be only too eager to lend an ear to the fallacies... it is the solemn duty of the Church to impart to these same peoples, so far as possible, the outstanding blessings of her life and her teaching, from which a new social order should be derived, based on Christian principles. Any delay or hesitation is full of danger; for the people of Africa have made as much progress toward civilization during the past few decades as required many centuries among the nations of Western Europe. Thus they are more easily unsettled and confused by the introduction of theoretical and applied scientific methods, with the result that they tend to be unduly inclined to a materialistic outlook on life. Hence a condition of affairs is sometimes brought about that is difficult to correct and in the course of time may prove to be a great obstacle to the growth of faith, whether in individuals or in society at large. For this reason it is imperative that help should be given now to the shepherds of the Lord's flock in order that their apostolic labours may correspond to the ever-growing needs of the times[10].

For centuries beginning with the crusades against the Moslems and later the strife and discord after the reformation, it was almost normal to hold in disdain those who did not share the same faith with the Catholic Church. The whole idea of salvation within the visible boundaries of the Roman Catholic Church in some way had a hand in shaping this view. As a way of preparing the ground for the ecumenical dialogue, in one of the first statements which almost suggested a fundamental shift in the line of thinking, Pope Pius IX went on to state that "God forbid that the children of the Catholic Church should even in any way be unfriendly to those who are not at all united to us by the same bonds of faith and love. On the contrary, let them be eager always to attend to their needs with all the kind services of Christian charity, whether they are poor or sick or suffering any other kind of visitation. First of all, let them rescue them from the darkness of the errors into which they have unhappily fallen and strive to guide them back to Catholic truth and to their most loving Mother who is ever holding out her maternal arms to receive them lovingly back into her fold. Thus, firmly founded in faith, hope, and charity and fruitful in every good work, they will gain eternal salvation"[11]

VATICAN II ERA

The latter part of the 1960's witnessed several upheavals in the social, political, economic and religious domains. It seems that over the years a certain degree of ferment had built up and was seeking release. Europe witnessed a series of political strikes, burnings and a continuous wave of civil disturbances that swept across the entire continent. While in the secular sphere the desire for change exhibited itself in the form of strikes and arson, this similar desire sought release in the calls for an ecumenical Council. The changes in the secular sphere brought almost a social quake while in the sacred realm a Church quake was inevitable. Up to the start of the second ecumenical Council, issues were very clear for many Catholics. The euphoria that marked the opening of the Council was unprecedented. Pope John XXIII could rightly say; "The Council now beginning rises in the Church like daybreak, a forerunner of most splendid light. It is now only dawn. And already at this first announcement of the rising day, how much sweetness fills our heart. Everything here breathes sanctity and arouses great joy. Let us contemplate the stars, which with their brightness augment the majesty of this temple. These stars, according to the testimony of the Apostle John (Apoc. 1:20), are you, and with you we see shining around the tomb of the Prince of the Apostles, the golden candelabra. That is, the Church is confided to you"[12] At the close of the Council the euphoria and hope dissipated leaving the progressive wing clamouring for more reforms while the conservative wing bemoaning the fate of a Church that was seen to be toying with errors with insidious and insipid experimentation. While it is true that every section of the Church was affected the field of missiology and ecclesiology witnessed nothing short of a revolution.

The question of precise boundaries of the Church and who belongs to the Church was given due attention by the Council Fathers. The dogmatic constitution of the Church "lumen Gentium states that "basing itself on sacred scriptures and tradition, the Council teaches that the Church, a pilgrim on earth, is necessary for salvation: the one Christ is the Mediator and the way of salvation, he is present to us in his body which is the Church. He himself explicitly asserted the necessity of the Church which men enter through baptism as through a door. Hence they could not be saved who, knowing that the Church [Catholic] was founded as necessary by God through Christ, would refuse to enter it or remain in it[13].

While not departing from the traditional teaching of the Church on salvation it went on to widen and clarify the teaching of the boundaries of the Church by adding that all humankind, are called by God's grace to salvation. Talking about the plan of salvation the Council stated that: "the plan of salvation also includes those who acknowledge the Creator. In the first place amongst these there are the Mohammedans, who, professing to hold the faith of Abraham, along with us adore the one and merciful God, who on the last day will judge humankind. Nor is God far distant from those who in shadows and images seek the unknown God, for it is He who gives to all men life and breath and all things, and as Saviour wills that all men be saved. Those also can attain to salvation who through no fault of their own do not know the Gospel of Christ or His Church, yet sincerely seek God and moved by grace strive by their deeds to do His will as it is known to them through the dictates of conscience. Nor does Divine Providence deny the helps necessary for salvation to those who, without blame on their part, have not yet arrived at an explicit knowledge of God and with His grace strive to live a good life. Whatever good or truth is found amongst them is looked upon by the Church as a preparation for the Gospel. She knows that it is given by Him who enlightens all men so that they may finally have life. But often men, deceived by the Evil One, have become vain in their reasoning and have exchanged the truth of God for a lie, serving the creature rather than the Creator.[14]

After discussing who can find salvation, the Council Fathers went on to define the boundaries of the Catholic Church. In the first phase "fully incorporated into the Church are those who, possessing the spirit of Christ, accept the means of salvation given to the Church together with all her entire organisation." The Church recognizes that in many ways she is linked with those who, being baptized, are honoured with the name of Christian, though they do not profess the faith in its entirety or do not preserve unity of communion with the successor of Peter. For there are many who honour Sacred Scripture, taking it as a norm of belief and a pattern of life, and who show a sincere zeal. They lovingly believe in God the Father Almighty and in Christ, the Son of God and Saviour. They are consecrated by baptism, in which they are united with Christ. They also recognize and accept other sacraments within their own Churches or ecclesiastical communities. Many of them rejoice in the episcopate, celebrate the Holy Eucharist and cultivate devotion toward the Virgin Mother of God. They also share with us in prayer and other spiritual benefits. Likewise we can say that in some real way they are joined with us in the Holy Spirit, for to them too He gives His gifts and graces whereby He is operative among them with His sanctifying power. Some indeed He has strengthened to the extent of the shedding of their blood. In all of Christ's disciples the Spirit arouses the desire to be peacefully united, in the manner determined by Christ, as one flock under one shepherd, and He prompts them to pursue this end. Mother Church never ceases to pray, hope and work that this may come about. She exhorts her children to purification and renewal so that the sign of Christ may shine more brightly over the face of the earth.[15]

The Council went on to profess its belief "that the Church is necessary for salvation, for Christ is the one Mediator and way of salvation and he becomes present to us in us in his body which is the Church. But the divine grace of salvation embraces all men. Those who are in ignorance of Christ's gospel and of his Church, through no fault of their own, who search for God in the sincerity of heart, and who acting according to conscience, strive under the influence of grace to fulfil his will, belong to his people, even though in a way we cannot see, and can obtain eternal salvation. Only God knows their number[16]. With respect to the way in which the salvific grace of God-, which is always given by means of Christ in the spirit and has a mysterious relationship with the Church-, comes to individual non-Christians, the second Vatican Council limited itself to the statement that God bestows it "in ways known to him. Theologians are seeking to understand this question more fully. Their work is to be encouraged, since it is certainly useful for understanding better God's salvific plan and the ways in which it is accomplished[17]

POLEMICS AND CONTROVERSIES SINCE VATICAN II

Did Lumen Gentium present a fundamental shift in thinking? Did theology of mission undergo a paradigm shift that had great repercussion for mission? Ever since the close of the Council many theologians have had to contend with this question. The number of documents issued since the close of the Council on the issue of mission leaves no one in doubt that all is not well. These storms that have rocked the Church since the close of the Council are well-known, and do not need lengthy rehearsal; the departure of thousands of priests and religious after the Council, the effective apostasy of many who remained, the vandalisation of the liturgy, the decline of religious practice among Catholics (amounting to an absolute decline in number in many places), the abandonment of catechesis on the basics of the faith, the general acceptance by Catholics of the moral standards of the unchristian society around them[18].

Forty years after the great ecumenical Council is enough time to allow for assessment of the repercussion of the Council's work. Did the Council's statement on the Church and salvation deal a grave blow to the early theology of mission, which had spurred so many young men and women in Europe to join the ranks of many Missionary Institutes and Societies of Apostolic Life? In The midst of this confusion the Congregation for Faith and Doctrine went on to clarify issues, which have often been debated by theologians. The five questions addressed by the congregation of the doctrine of the faith all touched on the understanding of the Church and mission.

Addressing the question, which has often been a source of polemics whether the Second Vatican Council changed the Catholic doctrine on the Church? The Second Vatican Council neither changed nor intended to change this doctrine; rather it developed, deepened and more fully explained it. This was exactly what John XXIII said at the beginning of the Council. Paul VI affirmed it and commented in the act of promulgating the Constitution Lumen Gentium: "There is no better comment to make than to say that this promulgation really changes nothing of the traditional doctrine. What Christ willed, we also will. What was still is. What the Church has taught down through the centuries, we also teach. In simple terms that which was assumed, is now explicit; that which was uncertain, is now clarified; that which was meditated upon, discussed and sometimes argued over, is now put together in one clear formulation"[19]. At beginning of the Council in the opening Address of 11 October 1962, Pope John XXIII went on to say "The Council...wishes to transmit Catholic doctrine, whole and entire, without alteration or deviation...To be sure, at the present time, it is necessary that Christian doctrine in its entirety, and with nothing taken away from it, is accepted with renewed enthusiasm, and serene and tranquil adherence... it is necessary that the very same doctrine be understood more widely and more profoundly as all those who sincerely adhere to the Christian, Catholic and Apostolic faith strongly desire ...it is necessary that this certain and unchangeable doctrine, to which is owed the obedience of faith, be explored and expounded in the manner required by our times. For the deposit of faith itself, or the truths which are contained in our venerable doctrine, are one thing; another thing is the way in which they are expressed, with however the same meaning and signification."

On the meaning of the affirmation that the Church of Christ subsists in the Catholic Church, the congregation went on to say Christ "established here on earth" only one Church and instituted it as a "visible and spiritual community" that from its beginning and throughout the centuries has always existed and will always exist, and in which alone are found all the elements that Christ himself instituted. "This one Church of Christ, which we confess in the Creed as one, holy, Catholic and apostolic [...]. This Church, constituted and organized in this world as a society, subsists in the Catholic Church, governed by the successor of Peter and the Bishops in communion with him."[20]

The congregation of the doctrine of faith went on to explain the word, subsistence. 'Subsistence' means this perduring, historical continuity and the permanence of all the elements instituted by Christ in the Catholic Church, in which the Church of Christ is concretely found on this earth. It is possible, according to Catholic doctrine, to affirm correctly that the Church of Christ is present and operative in the Churches and ecclesial Communities not yet fully in communion with the Catholic Church, on account of the elements of sanctification and truth that are present in them. Nevertheless, the word "subsists" can only be attributed to the Catholic Church alone precisely because it refers to the mark of unity that we profess in the symbols of the faith (I believe... in the "one" Church); and this "one" Church subsists in the Catholic Church.[21]

Why was the expression "subsists in" adopted instead of the simple word "is"? The use of this expression, which indicates the full identity of the Church of Christ with the Catholic Church, does not change the doctrine on the Church. Rather, it comes from and brings out more clearly the fact that there are "numerous elements of sanctification and of truth" which are found outside her structure, but which "as gifts properly belonging to the Church of Christ, impel towards Catholic Unity."[22]

"It follows that these separated Churches and Communities, though we believe they suffer from defects, are deprived neither of significance nor importance in the mystery of salvation. In fact, the Spirit of Christ has not refrained from using them as instruments of salvation, whose value derives from that fullness of grace and of truth which has been entrusted to the Catholic Church"[23]

Why does the Second Vatican Council use the term "Church" in reference to the oriental Churches separated from full communion with the Catholic Church? The Council wanted to adopt the traditional use of the term. "Because these Churches, although separated, have true sacraments and above all – because of the apostolic succession – the priesthood and the Eucharist, by means of which they remain linked to us by very close bonds" they merit the title of "particular or local Churches" and are called sister Churches of the particular Catholic Churches[24].

"It is through the celebration of the Eucharist of the Lord in each of these Churches that the Church of God is built up and grows in stature." However, since communion with the Catholic Church, the visible head of which is the Bishop of Rome and the Successor of Peter, is not some external complement to a particular Church but rather one of its internal constitutive principles, these venerable Christian communities lack something in their condition as particular Churches. On the other hand, because of the division between Christians, the fullness of universality, which is proper to the Church governed by the Successor of Peter and the Bishops in communion with him, is not fully realised in history. [25]

Why do the texts of the Council and those of the Magisterium since the Council not use the title of "Church" with regard to those Christian Communities born out of the Reformation of the sixteenth century? According to Catholic doctrine, these Communities do not enjoy apostolic succession in the sacrament of Orders, and are, therefore, deprived of a constitutive element of the Church. These ecclesial Communities, which, specifically because of the absence of the sacramental priesthood, have not preserved the genuine and integral substance of the Eucharistic Mystery, cannot, according to Catholic doctrine, be called "Churches" in the proper sense.[26]

The Second Vatican Council sought to renew the Church's life and activity in the light of the needs of the contemporary world. The Council emphasized the Church's "missionary nature," basing it in a dynamic way on the Trinitarian mission itself. The missionary thrust therefore belongs to the very nature of the Christian life, and is also the inspiration behind ecumenism: "that they may all be one...so that the world may believe that you have sent me" (Jn 17:21)[27].

The second Vatican Council is still at the heart of the struggles and fortunes of the Roman Catholic Church. Called with the purpose and expectation of bringing about growth and renewal in the Church –the 'new Pentecost' expected by Pope John XXII- it was followed by turmoil and catastrophe. It was precisely this shift in the theology of mission that caused missionary work to wane. Writing about the Council and its work Pope John Paul II gave a balanced account of the Council. Whereas many have blamed the Council for the present situation, he was keen to avoid the pitfall of giving any of the myopic extreme view of the Council. He gave a balanced view of the Council highlighting its strengths and weaknesses.

He began by recalling the fruits of the Council "The Council has already borne much fruit in the realm of missionary activity. There has been an increase in local Churches with their own bishops, clergy and workers in the apostolate. The presence of Christian communities is more evident in the life of nations, and communion between the Churches has led to a lively exchange of spiritual benefits and gifts. The commitment of the laity to the work of evangelization is changing ecclesial life, while particular Churches are more willing to meet with the members of other Christian Churches and other religions, and to enter into dialogue and cooperation with them. Above all, there is a new awareness that missionary activity is a matter for all Christians, for all dioceses and parishes, Church institutions and associations.[28]

After recalling the fruits of the Council he went on to say: "Nevertheless, in this "new springtime" of Christianity there is an undeniable negative tendency, and the present document is meant to help overcome it. Missionary activity specifically directed "to the nations" (ad gentes) appears to be waning, and this tendency is certainly not in line with the directives of the Council and of subsequent statements of the Magisterium. Difficulties both internal and external have weakened the Church's missionary thrust toward non-Christians, a fact which must arouse concern among all who believe in Christ. For in the Church's history, missionary drive has always been a sign of vitality, just as its lessening is a sign of a crisis of faith.[29]

Redemptoris Missio had as its sole aim interior renewal of faith and Christian life as a springboard for mission. Pope John Paul II stated the premise; "Twenty-five years after the conclusion of the Council and the publication of the Decree on Missionary Activity Ad Gentes, fifteen years after the Apostolic Exhortation Evangelii Nuntiandi issued by Pope Paul VI, and in continuity with the magisterial teaching of my predecessors, I wish to invite the Church to renew her missionary commitment. The present document has as its goal an interior renewal of faith and Christian life. For missionary activity renews the Church, revitalizes faith and Christian identity, and offers fresh enthusiasm and new incentive. Faith is strengthened when it is given to others! It is in commitment to the Church's universal mission that the new evangelization of Christian peoples will find inspiration and support.[30]

The traditional reason for mission, which the second Vatican Council sought to clarify, has remained one of the obstacles to surmount. If people can be saved without explicit proclamation of the gospel why mission in the first place. Pope John Paul II went on to say; "To the question, "why mission?" we reply with the Church's faith and experience that true liberation consists in opening oneself to the love of Christ. In him, and only in him, are we set free from all alienation and doubt, from slavery to the power of sin and death. Christ is truly "our peace" (Eph 2:14); "the love of Christ impels us" (2 Cor 5:14), giving meaning and joy to our life. Mission is an issue of faith, an accurate indicator of our faith in Christ and his love for us.[31]

The temptation today is to reduce Christianity to merely human wisdom, a pseudo-science of well-being. In our heavily secularized world a "gradual secularization of salvation" has taken place, so that people strive for the good of man, but man who is truncated, reduced to his merely horizontal dimension. We know, however, that Jesus came to bring integral salvation, one which embraces the whole person and all humankind, and opens up the wondrous prospect of divine filiations. Why mission? Because to us, as to St. Paul, "this grace was given to preach to the Gentiles the unsearchable riches of Christ" (Eph 3:8). Newness of life in him is the "Good News" for men and women of every age: all are called to it and destined for it. Indeed, all people are searching for it, albeit at times in a confused way, and have a right to know the value of this gift and to approach it freely. The Church, and every individual Christian within her, may not keep hidden or monopolize this newness and richness which has been received from God's bounty in order to be communicated to all humankind.[32]

Nevertheless, also as a result of the changes which have taken place in modern times and the spread of new theological ideas, some people wonder: Is missionary work among non-Christians still relevant? Has it not been replaced by inter-religious dialogue? Is not human development an adequate goal of the Church's mission? Does not respect for conscience and for freedom exclude all efforts at conversion? Is it not possible to attain salvation in any religion? Why then should there be missionary activity?

The decree on the Church's missionary activity went on to clarify the reason for mission Ad Gentes. "This missionary activity derives its reason from the will of God, "who wishes all men to be saved and to come to the knowledge of the truth. For there is one God, and one Mediator between God and men, Himself a man, Jesus Christ, who gave Himself as a ransom for all" (1 Tim. 2:45), "neither is there salvation in any other" (Acts 4:12). Therefore, all must be converted to Him, made known by the Church's preaching, and all must be incorporated into Him by baptism and into the Church which is His body. For Christ Himself "by stressing in express language the necessity of faith and baptism (cf. Mark 16:16; John 3:5), at the same time confirmed the necessity of the Church, into which men enter by baptism, as by a door. Therefore those men cannot be saved, who though aware that God, through Jesus Christ founded the Church as something necessary, still do not wish to enter into it, or to persevere in it." Therefore though God in ways known to Himself can lead those inculpably ignorant of the Gospel to find that faith without which it is impossible to please Him (Heb. 11:6), yet a necessity lies upon the Church (1 Cor. 9:16), and at the same time a sacred duty, to preach the Gospel. Hence missionary activity today as always retains its power and necessity [33]

Chapter Two: Missionary Theology

The missionary motives of the St. Joseph's society for foreign missions earlier had placed the number of those living in darkness and in the shadow of death at some nine hundred million people that was in the 1930s. "The Church, sent by Christ to reveal and to communicate the love of God to all men and nations, is aware that there still remains a gigantic missionary task for her to accomplish. For the Gospel message has not yet, or hardly yet, been heard by two million human beings (and their number is increasing daily), who are formed into large and distinct groups by permanent cultural ties, by ancient religious traditions, and by firm bonds of social necessity. Some of these men are followers of one of the great religions, but others remain strangers to the very knowledge of God, while still others expressly deny His existence, and sometimes even attack it. The Church, in order to be able to offer all of them the mystery of salvation and the life brought by God, must implant herself into these groups for the same motive which led Christ to bind Himself, in virtue of His Incarnation, to certain social and cultural conditions of those human beings among whom He dwelt'[34]

In recent years the urge and zeal to relaunch mission ad gentes have began to capture the interest and priority of the Church. "Missionary activity is nothing else and nothing less than an epiphany, or a manifesting of God's decree, and its fulfilment in the world and in world history, in the course of which God, by means of mission, manifestly works out the history of salvation. By the preaching of the word and by the celebration of the sacraments, the centre and summit of which is the most holy Eucharist, He brings about the presence of Christ, the author of salvation. But whatever truth and grace are to be found among the nations, as a sort of secret presence of God, He frees from all taint of evil and restores to Christ its maker, who overthrows the devil's domain and wards off the manifold malice of vice. And so, whatever good is found to be sown in the hearts and minds of men, or in the rites and cultures peculiar to various peoples, not only is not lost, but is healed, uplifted, and perfected for the glory of God, the shame of the demon, and the bliss of men. Thus, missionary activity tends toward eschatological fullness. For by it the people of God are increased to that measure and time, which the Father has fixed in His power(cf. Acts 1:7). To this people it was said in prophecy:

"Enlarge the space for your tent, and spread out your tent cloths unsparingly" (Is. 54:2). By missionary activity, the mystical body grows to the mature measure of the fullness of Christ (cf. Eph. 4:13); and the spiritual temple, where God is adored in spirit and in truth (cf. John 4:23), grows and is built up upon the foundation of the Apostles and prophets, Christ Jesus Himself being the supreme corner stone[35]

Nowadays the call to conversion, which missionaries address to non-Christians, is put into question or passed over in silence. It is seen as an act of "proselytizing"; it is claimed that it is enough to help people to become more human or more faithful to their own religion, that it is enough to build communities capable of working for justice, freedom, peace and solidarity. What is overlooked is that every person has the right to hear the "Good News" of the God who reveals and gives himself in Christ, so that each one can live out in its fullness his or her proper calling. This lofty reality is expressed in the words of Jesus to the Samaritan woman: "If you knew the gift of God," and in the unconscious but ardent desire of the woman: "Sir, give me this water, that I may not thirst" (Jn 4:10, 15).[36]

Inter-religious dialogue is a part of the Church's evangelising mission. Understood as a method and means of mutual knowledge and enrichment, dialogue is not in opposition to the mission ad gentes; indeed, it has special links with that mission and is one of its expressions. This mission, in fact, is addressed to those who do not know Christ and his Gospel, and who belong for the most part to other religions. In Christ, God calls all peoples to himself and he wishes to share with them the fullness of his revelation and love. He does not fail to make himself present in many ways, not only to individuals but also to entire peoples through their spiritual riches, of which their religions are the main and essential expression, even when they contain "gaps, insufficiencies and errors." All of this has been given ample emphasis by the Council and the subsequent Magisterium, without detracting in any way from the fact that salvation comes from Christ and that dialogue does not dispense from evangelization[37].

In the light of the economy of salvation, the Church sees no conflict between proclaiming Christ and engaging in inter religious dialogue. Instead, she feels the need to link the two in the context of her mission ad gentes. These two elements must maintain both their intimate connection and their distinctiveness; therefore they should not be confused, manipulated or regarded as identical, as though they were interchangeable.

Equality which is a presupposition of inter religious dialogue refers to the equal personal dignity of the parties in dialogue, not to the doctrinal content, nor even less to the person of Jesus Christ who is God himself made man in relations to the founders of other religions.[38]

Although the Church gladly acknowledges whatever is true and holy in the religious traditions of Buddhism, Hinduism and Islam as a reflection of that truth which enlightens all people, this does not lessen her duty and resolve to proclaim without fail Jesus Christ who is 'the way, and the truth and the life.' ...The fact that the followers of other religions can receive God's grace and be saved by Christ apart from the ordinary means which he has established does not thereby cancel the call to faith and baptism which God wills for all people." Indeed Christ himself "while expressly insisting on the need for faith and baptism, at the same time confirmed the need for the Church, into which people enter through Baptism as through a door." Dialogue should be conducted and implemented with the conviction that the Church is the ordinary means of salvation and that she alone possesses the fullness of the means of salvation.[39]

Furthermore, since the Church is the sign and instrument of salvation for all people, the opinion that the various religions are ways of salvation complementary to the Church is rejected as erroneous.[40]

Lastly, while recognizing that elements of truth and goodness exist in other religions, there are no grounds in Catholic theology for considering these religions as such as ways of salvation especially since they contain omissions, inadequacies and errors regarding fundamental truths about God, man and the world. Nor can their sacred texts be considered complementary to the Old Testament, which is the immediate preparation for the Christ event.[41]

In accordance with Catholic doctrine, it must be held that «whatever the Spirit brings about in human hearts and in the history of peoples, in cultures and religions, serves as a preparation for the

Gospel (cf. Dogmatic Constitution Lumen gentium, 16) It is therefore legitimate to maintain that the Holy Spirit accomplishes salvation in non-Christians also through those elements of truth and goodness present in the various religions; however, to hold that these religions, considered as such, are ways of salvation, has no foundation in Catholic theology, also because they contain omissions, insufficiencies and errors regarding fundamental truths about God, man and the world.[42]

There is today, however, a growing confusion which leads many to leave the missionary command of the Lord unheard and ineffective (cf. Mt 28:19). Often it is maintained that any attempt to convince others on religious matters is a limitation of their freedom. From this perspective, it would only be legitimate to present one's own ideas and to invite people to act according to their consciences, without aiming at their conversion to Christ and to the Catholic faith. It is enough, so they say, to help people to become more human or more faithful to their own religion; it is enough to build communities, which strive for justice, freedom, peace and solidarity. Furthermore, some maintain that Christ should not be proclaimed to those who do not know him, nor should joining the Church be promoted, since it would also be possible to be saved without explicit knowledge of Christ and without formal incorporation in the Church.[43]

Although non-Christians can be saved through the grace, which God bestows in "ways known to him", the Church cannot fail to recognize that such persons are lacking a tremendous benefit in this world: to know the true face of God and the friendship of Jesus Christ, God-with-us. Indeed "there is nothing more beautiful than to be surprised by the Gospel, by the encounter with Christ. There is nothing more beautiful than to know him and to speak to others of our friendship with him." The revelation of the fundamental truths about God, about the human person and the world, is a great good for every human person, while living in darkness without the truths about ultimate questions is an evil and is often at the root of suffering and slavery, which can at times be devastating. This is why Saint Paul does not hesitate to describe conversion to the Christian faith as liberation "from the power of darkness" and entrance into "the kingdom of his beloved Son in whom we have redemption and the forgiveness of our sins" (Col 1:13-14). Therefore, fully belonging to Christ, who is the Truth, and entering the Church do not lessen human freedom, but rather exalt it and direct it towards its fulfilment, in a love that is freely given and which overflows with care for the good of all people. It is an inestimable benefit to live within the universal embrace of the friends of God, which flows from communion in the life-giving flesh of his Son, to receive from him the certainty of forgiveness of sins and to live in the love that is born of faith. The Church wants everyone to share in these goods so that they may possess the fullness of truth and the fullness of the means of salvation, in order "to enter into the freedom of the glory of the children of God" (Rom 8:21)[44].

However, the Church's "missionary proclamation is endangered today by relativistic theories which seek to justify religious pluralism, not only de facto but also de iure (or in principle)." For a long time, the reason for evangelization has not been clear to many among the Catholic faithful. It is even stated that the claim to have received the gift of the fullness of God's revelation masks an attitude of intolerance and a danger to peace.[45]

Those who make such claims are overlooking the fact that the fullness of the gift of truth, which God makes by revealing himself to man, respects the freedom which he himself created as an indelible mark of human nature: a freedom which is not indifference, but which is rather directed towards truth. This kind of respect is a requirement of the Catholic faith itself and of the love of Christ; it is a constitutive element of evangelization and, therefore, a good, which is to be promoted inseparably with the commitment to making the fullness of salvation, which God offers to the human race in the Church, known and freely embraced[46].

Theology is proving even more important in times of great cultural and spiritual change like ours which, in raising new problems and questions concerning the Church's consciousness of her faith, require new answers and solutions, even daring ones. One cannot deny that today the presence of religious pluralism obliges Christians to look with a renewed awareness at the place of other religions in the saving plan of the Triune God. In this context, theology is called upon to give a response which, in the light of Revelation and the

Church's Magisterium, will justify the significance and value of other religious traditions, which have shown a renewed central role in guiding and motivating the lives of millions of people in every part of the world. [47]

With regard to the universal salvific action of the Holy Spirit, it reinstated that the Spirit working after Jesus' resurrection is always the Spirit of Christ sent by the Father, who works in a salvific way also outside the visible Church. It is therefore contrary to the Catholic faith to hold that the Holy Spirit's salvific action may be more extensive than the one universal salvific economy of the incarnate Word. Furthermore, since the Church is sign and instrument of salvation for all people, the opinion that the various religions are ways of salvation complementary to the Church is rejected as erroneous. Lastly, while recognizing that elements of truth and goodness exist in other religions, there are no grounds in Catholic theology for considering these religions as such as ways of salvation especially since they contain omissions, inadequacies and errors regarding fundamental truths about God, man and the world. Nor can their sacred texts be considered complementary to the Old Testament, which is the immediate preparation for the Christ event.[48]

The Congregation for the Doctrine of the Faith, on January 24, 2001, published the NOTIFICATION on the book Toward a Christian Theology of Religious Pluralism by Father JACQUES DUPUIS, S.J. Beneath are some of the points which have been a source of confusion since the close of the Council. There is no better way to conclude this reflection than with the final recommendations arrived at by this congregation.

It must be firmly believed that Jesus Christ, the Son of God made man, crucified and risen, is the sole and universal Mediator of salvation for all humanity It must also be firmly believed that Jesus of Nazareth, Son of Mary and only Saviour of the world, is the Son and Word of the Father. For the unity of the divine plan of salvation centred in Jesus Christ, it must also be held that the salvific action of the Word is accomplished in and through Jesus Christ, the Incarnate Son of the Father, as Mediator of salvation for all humanity. It is therefore contrary to the Catholic faith not only to posit a separation between the Word and Jesus, or between the

Word's salvific activity and that of Jesus, but also to maintain that there is a salvific activity of the Word as such in his divinity, independent of the humanity of the Incarnate Word.

It must be firmly believed that Jesus Christ is the Mediator, the fulfilment and the completeness of revelation. It is therefore contrary to the Catholic faith to maintain that revelation in Jesus Christ (or the revelation of Jesus Christ) is limited, incomplete or imperfect. Moreover, although full knowledge of divine revelation will be had only on the day of the Lord's coming in glory, the historical revelation of Jesus Christ offers everything necessary for man's salvation and has no need of completion by other religions. It is consistent with Catholic doctrine to hold that the seeds of truth and goodness that exist in other religions are a certain participation in truths contained in the revelation of or in Jesus Christ. However, it is erroneous to hold that such elements of truth and goodness, or some of them, do not derive ultimately from the source-mediation of Jesus Christ.

The Church's faith teaches that the Holy Spirit, working after the resurrection of Jesus Christ, is always the Spirit of Christ sent by the Father, who works in a salvific way in Christians as well as non-Christians. It is therefore contrary to the Catholic faith to hold that the salvific action of the Holy Spirit extends beyond the one universal salvific economy of the Incarnate Word.

It must be firmly believed that the Church is sign and instrument of salvation for all people. It is contrary to the Catholic faith to consider the different religions of the world as ways of salvation complementary to the Church. According to Catholic doctrine, the followers of other religions are oriented to the Church and are all called to become part of her.

In accordance with Catholic doctrine, it must be held that «whatever the Spirit brings about in human hearts and in the history of peoples, in cultures and religions, serves as a preparation for the Gospel (cf. Dogmatic Constitution Lumen gentium, 16). It is therefore legitimate to maintain that the Holy Spirit accomplishes salvation in non-Christians also through those elements of truth and goodness present in the various religions; however, to hold that these religions, considered as such, are ways of salvation, has no foundation in Catholic theology, also because they contain omissions, insufficiencies and errors regarding fundamental truths about God, man and the world.

Notes

1. Benedict XV. Maximum Illud: Apostolic Letter on the Propagation of the Faith Throughout the world. 30 November 1919. Translated by Thomas J. M. Burke, SJ Washington, DC: National Catholic Welfare Office.

2. Cf David J. Bosch (1991) Transforming Mission Paradigm Shifts on Theology of Mission Orbis books New York.

3. ibid.

4. Ibid p.211.

5. Benedict XV. Maximum Illud: Apostolic Letter on the Propagation of the Faith Throughout the world. 30 November 1919. Translated by Thomas J. M. Burke, SJ Washington, DC: National Catholic Welfare Office, no. 6.

6. Pope Pius XII, Ad Apostolorum Principis Encyclical letter on Communism and the Church in China no.46.

7. Constitutions of St. Joseph's Society for Foreign Mission, 1930.

8. Pope Pius IX, Promotion of false doctrines, August 10, 1863 no.7.

9. Ibid no.6.

10. Pope Pius XII Fidei Donum no.21-22.

11. Ibid.

12. On October 11, 1962, the first day of the Council, Pope John XXIII delivered this address in St. Peter's Basilica.

13. Lumen gentium.

14. Second Vatican Council, Dogmatic Constitution Lumen Gentium,16.

15. Second Vatican Council, Dogmatic constitution lumen Gentium 17.

16. Paul, VI,(1968) The Credo of the People of God.

17. Congregation for the Doctrine of Faith (2000) Iesus Dominus, Declaration on the Unicity and Salvific Universality of Jesus Christ and the Church.

18. Cf Schreck, Alan, Vatican II: The Crisis and the Promise, Ralph McInerny, What Went Wrong With Vatican II: The Catholic Crisis Explained, Jean Lamont: what went wrong with Vatican II.

19. Congregation for the Doctrine of the Faith, (2007) Responses to Some Questions Regarding Aspects of the Doctrine of the Church.
20. Ibid.
21. Ibid.
22. Ibid.
23. Ibid.
24. Ibid.
25. Ibid.
26. Congregation for the Doctrine of the Faith (2007) Responses to Some Questions Regarding Aspects of the Doctrine of the Church.
27. John Paul II, (1990) Encyclical Letter, Redemptoris Missio, on the Mission of the Redeemer, Vatican.
28. Ibid.
29. Ibid.
30. Ibid.
31. Ibid.
32. Ibid.
33. Vatican II (1968) Decree on the Mission Activity of the Church Ad Gentes Divinitus.
34. Ibid.
35. Ibid.
36. Ibid no. 46.
37. Ibid no. 55.
38. Congregation of the Doctrine of Faith, Iesus Dominus op. cit, no.22.
39. Ibid.
40. Ibid.
41. Ibid.
42. Ibid.
43. Congregation for the Doctrine of the Faith.(2000) Doctrinal Notes on Some Aspects of Evangelisation.

44. Ibid.
45. Ibid.
46. Commentary on the Notification of the Congregation for the Doctrine of the Faith regarding the book Toward a Christian Theology of Religious pluralism by Father Jacques Dupuis, S.J.
47. Ibid.
48. Ibid.

CHAPTER THREE
MOTIVES AND METHODS

INTRODUCTION

The history of humanity has known many major turning points which have encouraged missionary outreach, and the Church, guided by the spirit, has always responded to them with generosity and farsightedness[1]. One of these major turning points was colonisation of Cameroon by the Germans in 1884. The Mill hill missionaries who took over from the Pallotine and Sacred Heart Missionaries evangelised most of the present day Anglophone Cameroon. They took advantage of a specific historical development just as their predecessors, the Pallotine and the sacred Heart Fathers, had done when in 1923 following the partition of Cameroon and the signing of the agreement partitioning Cameroon between the British and the French accepted from the Holy See the task of taking over the reins of the departing Pallotine Missionaries.

Missionary activity does not operate in a vacuum. It makes use of methods and tools hewed out of human experience. The Mill Hill missionaries used several methods which had been applied elsewhere in the world to evangelise Cameroon. The methods used were not out of the blues. The methodology used to further the cause of Christianity were not born in isolation, they were a product of history refined over the centuries. Methods of evangelisation used by the Catholic Church have varied over the centuries. To a modern thinker some of these methods may seem barbaric, and in some cases violent enough even to cause outrage. It is proper to make a clear distinction between the methods employed to force former Catholics into the sheepfold and the methods used to woo those who were never Christians at all to become Christians. A historical survey of these methods, from the apostolic times to the patristic time, the medieval age up to the evangelisation of Africa reveals no uniform pattern.

MISSIONARY METHODS
APOSTLIC AND PATRISTIC ERA

Up to the time of Constantine, Christianity remained largely a religion of the minority suffering under the weight of scorn, persecution and rejection. The apologetics of the first century fought through persuasion to win people over to Christ Jesus. Beginning with the apostle Paul, preaching and writing were the principal tools of evangelisation. Paul's strategy was to preach first to the Jews in every town he went to before he could turn his attention to the gentiles.

The persecution of the Christians in the second century was largely local, conducted according to the zeal of the local imperial authorities. Nevertheless, the persecutions were widespread and the Christians were generally hated even by the most tolerant and open-minded of the Roman rulers. They were hated mostly for what was considered their stubbornness and intolerance due to their exclusive devotion to Christ as Lord. They were persecuted also for what was considered to be the political danger which they brought to the unity of law and order in the imperial reign, particularly because of the increasing number of persons who were joining the Church.

The Christians were criminals in the eyes of the Romans, not only religiously, but also politically. They transgressed the laws of the state because they refused to honour the earthly emperor as king, lord, and god, which was required of them as members of imperial society. They prayed for the civil authorities and gave "honour to whom honour is due" (Romans 13:1-7), but they refused to give the earthly king the glory and worship which was due to God, and to His Christ, alone. Thus the Roman law declared: It is not lawful to be a Christian.

In the third century in the Epistle to Diognetus the writer went on to say: Christians are not to be distinguished from the rest of mankind by either country, speech, or customs; the fact is, they nowhere settle in the cities of their own; they use no particular language of their own; they cultivate no eccentric mode of life. Certainly this creed of theirs is no discovery due doctrine of human origin… They love all men yet they are persecuted by all. They are unknown yet are condemned; they are put to death, yet is life that they receive. They are reviled yet they bless[2].

Chapter Three: Motives and Methods

The Edict of Milan was issued in AD 313, in the names of the Emperor Constantine, who ruled the western parts of the empire, and Licinius, who ruled the East. A previous edict of toleration had been recently issued by the Emperor Galerius from Serdica and posted up at Nicomedia on 13 May 311. By its provisions, the Christians, who had "followed such a caprice and had fallen into such a folly that they would not obey the institutes of antiquity", were granted an indulgence.

It directed the provincial magistrates to execute this order at once with all energy, so that public order may be restored and the continuance of the Divine favour may "preserve and prosper our successes together with the good of the state."

The Church in a very short time following the change of events turned from being persecuted to be the persecutor. Although Constantine never made Christianity the official religion of his empire he encouraged all citizens to become Christians. His reign marked the ascendancy of Christianity to officialdom. He gave Christian bishops the authority of judges in their dioceses, exempted Church estate from taxation, gave money to needy congregations, built several Churches in Constantinople and throughout the empire forbade the worship of images in the new capital.

Although Constantine officially supported Christianity, outlawing heretical religions he himself did not become a Christian until he was almost in his deathbed. In 337, at the age of sixty-four, he put on the garb of the Christian neophyte, finally received baptism and passed away[3]. Much has been written about the harm done to the cause of the gospel when Constantine accepted baptism, and it is not difficult to expatiate on this theme. It is easy to see with hindsight how quickly the Church fell into the temptation of worldly power and into compromise with the world. The once vibrant, militant Church keeping faith even under the weight of persecution was soon diluted with the spirit of the world.

After 400AD, St. Augustine gradually came to the conviction that external pressure had a role to play. To provide the individual with the opportunity to flee eternal damnation could not be wrong and certainly justified the use of pressure but Augustine confined coercive methods to fines, confiscation of property and even exile. Taking the cue from the Gospel according to Luke 14:23 it is said:

"go out to the country roads and lanes and make people come in, so that my house will be full." He went on to say: "I myself have yielded to the evidence afforded by these instances which my colleagues have laid before me. For originally my opinion was that no one should be coerced into the unity of Christ, and that we must act only by words, fight only by arguments, and prevail by force of reason, lest we should have those whom we knew as avowed heretics feigning themselves to be Catholics. But this opinion of mine was overcome, not by the word of those who controverted it, but by the conclusive instance to which they could point[4].

There is a persecution of unrighteousness, which the impious inflict upon the Church of Christ, but there is a righteous persecution which the Church of Christ inflicts upon the impious. Moreover, she persecutes in the spirit of love, while they in the spirit of wrath. Wherefore, if the power which the Church received by divine providence is due season, through the religiosity and the faith of Emperors, be the instrument by which those on the highways and at the hedges- that is those in heresies and schisms- are compelled to come in, then let them find no fault with being compelled, but concede to what they are being so compelled: it is to the Supper of the Lord, which is the unity of the Body of Christ.[5]

With the articulation of the views of Augustine and gradual imbibing of this mentality, the Church embarked on a series of methods whose main aim was to forced people to become Christians. Gregory the great, two centuries later sanctioned the use of subtle methods to force non-Christians to accept baptism. He admonished Sardinian landowners that their peasant labourers were to be overburdened with rent; that the weight of this punitive exaction should make them hasten to righteousness. This was not all; those who were adamant and would stubbornly refuse to become Christians were to be chastised by beating and torture. This was the lot of slaves, but for those who were freemen they were to be jailed. Among the methods that were used in the Middle Ages to coerce people to become Christians was the granting or withdrawal of rights. Non-Christians did not have the same rights as Christians and once they were baptised they were granted the same political rights as their fellow Christians. It was therefore politically and economically advantageous to become Christian.

Already in the second or third century, Christianity was carried to the Britons and the Germans on the borders of the Rhine. But these were sporadic efforts with transient results. The work did not begin in earnest till the sixth century and then it went vigorously forward to the tenth and twelfth, though with many checks and temporal lapses caused by civil wars and foreign invasions. In the Middle Ages the Jews became the object of the Church's missionary efforts. The method and efforts at converting the Jews were not very different from those used against the heretics. Those who refused to convert to Christianity were sometimes threatened with expulsion and even execution. It was Pope Gregory the great who opted for the contrary. For him Jews were to be brought to the Christian faith by mildness, generosity and persuasion.

MEDIAVAL AGE

Medieval Christianisation was a wholesale conversion or a conversion of nations under the command of their leaders. It was carried on not only by the missionaries and by spiritual means, but also by political influence, alliances of heathen princes with Christian wives, and in some cases by military force. It was a conversion not to the primary Christianity inspired by the apostles as laid down in the New Testament but to the secondary Christianity of ecclesiastical tradition as taught by the Fathers of the Church, monks and Popes. It was a baptism by water rather than by the fire and the Holy Spirit. The preceding instructions amounted to little or nothing; even the baptismal formula, mechanically recited in Latin, was scarcely understood. The rude barbarians, owing to the weakness of their heathen religion, readily submitted to the new religion; but some tribes yielded to the sword of the conqueror. The superficial, wholesale conversion to nominal Christianity must be regarded in the light of the infant baptism.[6]

The missionaries of the Middle Ages were nearly all monks. They were generally men of limited education and narrow views, but of devoted zeal and heroic self denial. Accustomed to primitive simplicity of life, detached from all earthly ties, trained to all sorts of deprivations, ready for any amount of labour and commanding attention and veneration by their unusual habits, their celibacy, fasting and constant devotions, they were upon the whole the best pioneers of Christianity and civilisations among the savage races of northern and western Europe[7].

The conversion of Russia followed the way of other nations in Europe. Vladimir sent emissaries to both Rome and Constantinople to see the religions at work. The visitors to Constantinople were overwhelmed with the grandeur and splendour of the services at the majestic Church of St. Sophia and thus highly recommended eastern orthodoxy. Vladimir was baptised in 988. His twelve sons followed his example, and the Russian people accepted Christianity en Masse. When enough priests could not be found to baptise them, thousands lined up at the River Kiev and immersed themselves. Russia thus entered Christendom in 989. Russia began to lift itself out of its barbarism to establish the beginning of a great civilisation which was to stand the test of time[8].

THE AGE OF EXPLORATION AND COLONISATION

With the dawn of the era of exploration, discovery and colonisation the Christian world discovered with shock that after fifteen centuries of evangelisation there were still millions of people who knew nothing of salvation and who because they were not baptised were heading for eternal damnation. Colonisation of the non Christian people by a Christian nation was not new. In earlier centuries it was a European nation colonising a European nation where the conquered people accepted Christianity and were assimilated into the prevailing culture of the time. What was essentially new with the new wave of colonisation of the sixteenth century was the colonisation of the people who had a different colour, language and culture different from that of the colonising power.

However, with the European expansion into the new world, the dark page of slavery was opened. Slavery was not new. It is as old as the history of man's attempt to dominate his fellow man and bring him under his command. Under the Roman Empire and up to the sixteenth century slavery had nothing to do with race or colour of the skin. However once the new world was discovered the colour bar began to manifest itself in the most ferocious and vicious form. Only people of the "inferior" race could become slaves. This had consequences for mission as we shall see later an issue that persisted well into the twentieth century and even beyond.

Bartolome de las Casas (1478-1566) the Dominican missionary to Latin America confronted the centuries –old idea that violence was the way to convert people to Christianity. As a pastor, he developed advice for missionaries that is relevant today. He rejected the horrible lie that the atrocities of conquest and exploitation were the way to convert people. He wrote that Jesus Christ did not give his apostles "power to punish the unwilling by any force, pressure or harshness."

In September, 1510, Pedro de Cordova, landed with the first band of Dominicans in Hispaniola. He was the first, in 1511, to denounce publicly in America the enslavement and oppression of the Indians as sinful and disgraceful to the Spanish nation. Being censured for this, he was forcefully sent home to Spain in 1512, where he pleaded the cause of the Indians so successfully that the king took immediate measures towards ameliorating their condition.

In December 1511, a Dominican preacher Father Friar Antonio de Montessino preached a fiery sermon that implicated the colonists in the genocide of the native peoples. He is said to have preached, "Tell me by what right of justice do you hold these Indians in such a cruel and horrible servitude? On what authority have you waged such detestable wars against these people who dealt quietly and peacefully on their own lands? Wars in which you have destroyed such an infinite number of them by homicides and slaughters never heard of before. Why do you keep them so oppressed and exhausted, without giving them enough to eat or curing them of the sicknesses they incur from the excessive labour you give them, and they die, or rather you kill them, in order to extract and acquire gold every day."

The early missionaries to Latin America had the most unfortunate task of preaching to a people enslaved by their own countrymen. How were they to convince the natives of these countries of the need to be saved when their fellow countrymen were the very persons whose practice of religion was mere religiosity, not more than skin deep? Missionaries depended on the very colonisers for help and protection and even finance. With the introduction of the patronage system missionaries had to walk on a tightrope. It was tantamount to biting the hand that fed them.

In 1492, the same year the Moors were expelled from Spain, Columbus made his historic voyage to the America. Within the next three decades Global Exploration was expanded by the various voyages of Vasca Da Gama who reached India around the Cape of Good Hope in 1498 after which additional explorations by the Portuguese were made into the Indian Ocean, the Red Sea, the Persian Gulf, and into the Pacific Ocean where they made landfall in Japan in 1543.

Throughout the early 16th Century the rulers of Western Europe were financing the exploration of the globe with dreams of expanded empires as their motive. The impetus toward building empires set much of the stage for the drama of St. Francis Xavier missionary efforts to Japan. Not only was St. Francis Xavier's selected as the head of missions to Asia for the Jesuit Order but he also represented the Crown of Portugal as a political emissary.

Arriving in Japan in 1549, Francis Xavier and his companions began their work of spreading the gospel in a land where Buddhism and Shintoism were the predominant religions. One of Xavier's companions described some of their methods in the following words; " we preached in the streets without any licence or permission of the king, taking up our position at cross roads where people thronged ...some merely listened to kill time, others to have their ears tickled with novelties, and many more just to make a sport of us. A few showed us marks of affection and pity."[9]

In 1537, the Pope used his temporal and spiritual power to authorise the opening of a slave market in Lisbon where Africans were sold annually for transportation to the West Indies. Slave trade and evangelisation went hand in hand. With the discovery of the sea route to India Pope Alexander VI divided the world outside Europe between the king of Portugal and Spain, granting them full authority over all the territories they had discovered as well as those still to be discovered. Here lies the origin of the right of the patronage according to which rulers of the two countries i.e. Spain and Portugal had dominion over their colonies not only in political matters but also in the spiritual and Church matters. The ruling by which the king of Spain and Portugal were made patrons of the missionary expansions in their colonies made the propagation of faith and colonial policies so intertwined that it was often hard if not impossible to distinguish the one from the other. Bishops could only be appointed with the king's approval and could not communicate with the Pope directly. In the Papal Bull Inter Caetera on the 4th of May 1493 Pope Alexander VI wrote "we therefore are rightly led and hold it as our duty, to grant you even of our own accord and in your favour those things whereby with effort each day hearty you may be enabled for the honour of God himself and the spread of the Christian rule to carry forward your holy and praiseworthy purpose so pleasing to immortal God...and in order that you may enter upon so great an undertaking with greater readiness and heartiness endowed with the benefit of our apostolic favour, we, of our own accord not at your instance nor the request of anyone else in your regard but out of our sole largess and certain knowledge and out of fullness of our apostolic power, by the authority of the almighty God conferred upon us in blessed Peter .. said islands that have been found by your envoys and captains, give, grant and assign to you and your heirs and successors, forever together with all their dominions cities camps, places and villages and all rights, jurisdictions and appurtenances, all islands mainland found and to be found."[10]

The creation of the patronage system was in the years to come to prove fatal to the Church itself. In some cases Rome only became an observer as the powerful monarchs of Spain and Portugal determined not only the colonial policy but also the missionary policies to be followed as well as the missionaries to be sent or approved for missions. To forestall such a situation, the Church responded by creating the Sacred Congregation for the Propagation of Faith where the entire missionary activity and efforts were directly assigned exclusively to the Pope.

In 1926, Pope Pius XI in his Encyclical Rerum Ecclesiae on the missions addressed many issues, which were of particular importance for African Churches. Apart from determining the missionary policies of the colonies, the king of Spain forbade the training of natives as Priests, thus the indigenes saw the Church as a foreign institution in which they would always be second-class members. Pope Pius went on to say: "Anyone who looks upon these natives as members of an inferior race or as men of low mentality makes a grievous mistake. Experience over a long period of time has proven that the inhabitants of those remote regions of the East and of the South frequently are not inferior to us at all, and are capable of holding their own with us, even in mental ability. If one discovers an extreme lack of the ability to understand among those who live in the very heart of certain barbarous countries, this is largely due to the conditions under which they exist, for since their daily needs are so limited, they are not often called upon to make use of their intellects. You, Venerable Brothers and Beloved Sons, can bear testimony to the truth of what we write, and we Ourselves can testify to these facts since We have here under Our very eyes the example of certain native students attending the colleges of Rome who not only are equal to the other students in ability and in the results they obtain in their studies, but frequently even surpass them.. Therefore, there should exist no discrimination of any kind between priests, be they European missionaries or natives, there must be no line of demarcation marking one off from the other. Let all priests, missionaries and natives be united with one another in the bonds of mutual respect and love. [11]

MOTIVES OF CONVERSION TO CHRISTIANITY
INTRODUCTION

The question why Africans became Christians has always been of interest to mission studies. Were there some deficiencies in African Traditional Religion that Africans wanted to remedy by joining the new religion? The answer may not be in the affirmative. Ordinary Africans saw little need for a new religion since they already perceived themselves as spiritually self-contained, in a life comprehensively regulated by custom and tradition. Although termed pagan, the people of Southern Nigeria followed a well-developed form of traditional religion. There were differences of belief and practices from tribe to tribe and often from village to village but there were many common elements such as the existence of a High God and a number of lesser deities. The predominant Ibo tribe called their High God Chukwu but also venerated, among others, a sun-god, a storm-god and an earth-goddess who was depicted in statues reminiscent of the Christian Madonna. There were simple hut-temples to various deities, and numerous shrines, many of them honouring family ancestors. There were oracles, too, which were used to settle dispute and provide direction in times of difficulty. The most famous of these was a sinister cave at Arochukwu known as the long Juju. Ibos came from far and wide to consult this oracle and it became a symbol of unity and integration for the tribe[12]. Christianity was often fiercely resisted in many localities and where it was accepted it was often for ulterior motives. Africans were in many ways religiously self-contained.

It was the missionary who saw deficiencies in African Traditional Religion and not the African himself. Elders after listening to the good news advised Shanahan to tell it to the children. This scenario was not a privilege of the people of southern Nigeria but a common and regular feature of all African societies. This hangover of this religious sufficiency continues to lurk in the back of the mind of the African and has been and remains one of the constant temptations to the African to return to his roots in times of crisis and the most benign problem that Christianity has not succeeded in surmounting. This degree of self-sufficiency in religious matters was and has been prevalent not only in the minds of Africans but also in all non-Christian religions the world over. A historical survey of the motives and methods of conversions to Christianity over the centuries presents some interesting facts.

APOSTOLIC AND PATRISTIC ERA

Over the centuries, people in various countries have embraced Christianity for various reasons under very different circumstances. In the first century, Conversions were sparked of by apostolic preaching and miracles. The first conversion at Pentecost and later the miracles performed through the apostles were the main reasons for the conversions of the first century. Christianity at this time was a religion struggling to free itself from Judaism and suffering under persecution. Cyril (315-387), Bishop of Jerusalem in his famous work of twenty-four catechetical lectures, which he gave in the Basilica of the Holy Sepulchre, was not deceived by the variety of motivations among the candidates. "Possibly you have come on another pretext. It is possible that a man is wishing to pay court to a woman and came on that account. This remark applies in like manner to women also in their turn. Perhaps a slave wishes to please his master, and a friend his friend I accept this bait for the hook and welcome you, though you came with ill purpose, yet as one to be stayed by a good hope. Perhaps you do not know where you are coming or in what kind of net you were taken[13]. Up to the time of Emperor Constantine Christianity was a religion of the minority. From that time onwards it gradually moved from being a religion of the minority to being a religion of the majority. How Christianity became a main line religion was as a result of many factors (some coercive) that have been used over the centuries for people to become Christians. Thus with the help of civil legislation, state power Europe gradually became Christian.

THE REFORMATION

The saying that Religion follows the crown became evident when the Catholic Church lost its control and monopoly of the religions sphere with the onset of Protestant Reformation. Even before the reformation the subjects often followed the religion of their crown. However, after the reformation it ceased to be only a matter of Christianity with other religions but a matter of denominations. Nowhere was this more evident than in England. Under Henry VIII and Edward VI, England made great strides on the path of Protestantism. However, under Mary the story was different. Mary pressed England's return to Catholicism with fanatical zeal. She executed about three hundred protestant leaders. So numerous were the beheadings and burnings during her reign that she became known as "bloody Mary."

But it was in Germany, the birthplace of the reformation that the rule, religion follows the crown, was officially accepted. In 1555, an assembly of German Catholics and Lutherans agreed to the peace of Augsburg which said that the local ruler could choose the religion of his domain. From then on German provinces generally followed the belief of the local Duke or Prince. By the early 1550s it was apparent that a negotiated settlement was necessary. In 1555 the peace of Augsburg was signed. The settlement, which represented a victory for the princes granted recognition to both Lutheranism and Catholicism in German, and each ruler gained the right to decide the religion to be practised within his state. Subjects of this faith could move to another state with their property and disputes between the religions were to be settled in court.

AGE OF EXPLORATION AND COLONISATION

Outside Europe, with the discovery of the new world, the motives for natives converting to Christianity took central stage. The Jesuit missionaries were the bearers of the gospel message in many of the Spanish colonies. The Indians became Christian for a number of reasons: first, many of the missionaries were good to them. The friars generally took an educational approach; they learned the native language, constructed alphabets and wrote catechism to teach the faith. Some of the natives believed that the Christian God must be stronger than their own because the Spaniards had conquered the native people, if the Indians converted they would be on the winning side and in addition they would have something in common with the Spaniards. Finally some Indians believed in the Christian faith. The motives were nothing new to Christianity. In many ways these were very similar to the three reasons that had motivated the European tribes of the Goths, Vandals, and Franks to convert to Christianity many centuries before.

The motives for African converting to Christianity were very similar. African literature alludes to some of these motives. Chinua Achebe in Arrow of God in describing the early encounter between the village of Umuaro and Christianity goes on to highlight some of their motivations. The chief priest, who was the custodian of the tribal religion, sent his son to school for very ulterior motives. "The world is fast changing' he had told him' I do like it. But I am like the bird Eneke-nti-oba. When his friend asked him why he was always on wings he replied: "men of today have learnt to shoot without missing and so I have learnt to fly without perching" I want my sons to join these people and be my eye there. If there is nothing in it you will come back. But if there was something there you will bring home my share. The world is like a mask dancing. If you want to see it well you do not stand in one place. My spirit tells me that those who do not befriend the Whiteman today will be saying had we known tomorrow. Do you not know that in the great man's household there must be people who follow all kinds of strange ways?"

These motives were not completely unfounded. Early Missionaries in some cases presented Christianity as a gateway to a better life not just in heaven but the heaven was to begin here on earth with material benefit accruing from well paid employment. While enticing the village chief to send their children to school, Shanahan proposed the advantages that will come with the school. The children of your town will come to that house everyday to learn about Chuckwu. They will also learn book there and will know more than the children of other towns. After some years in that house-for-book, they will be fit for government work and will make much money.[14]

Shanahan in his attempt to woo the Ibos to Christianity frequently presented education as bait. It was founded on the belief that it was very difficult to achieve large scale conversion among adults whose minds were already formed. They were also entangled in a web of tribal relationship which made a sudden change in lifestyle very difficult. School would act as a fertile ground for them to listen to the doctrine. They will later be examined on their Christian faith and commitment. Once they were baptised, they will form the nucleus of the Church and later to form Christian families once marriage had taken place in the Church. They will form their Christian community, their own parish around their own school and Church and priest. It was so simple but there were many 'ifs'[15]

The motives for embracing Christianity were mixed. It seems to have been almost a universal phenomenon that did not cease to baffle even some of the early missionaries. Seeing the world through the eyes of Reverend Father Superior Drumont, Mongo Beti addresses similar worries "why do you think that so many backslide from true religion? Why did they come to Mass in the first place? The catechist answered: Father. The first of us who ran to religion, to your religion, came to it as a sort of ...revelation. Yes, that's it, a revelation; a school where they could learn your secret, the secret of your power, of your aeroplanes and railways...in a word, the secret of your mystery. Instead of that, you began talking to them of God, of the soul, of eternal life, and so forth. Do you really suppose they didn't know those things already, long before you came? So of course, they decided that you were hiding something. Later, they saw that if they had money they could get plenty of things for themselves – gramophones and cars, and perhaps even aeroplanes one day. Well, then! They are turning from religion and running elsewhere, after money, no less. That's the truth of it, Father.

As for the rest, it's all make-believe...' seemingly confronted by fear of his apparent failure, the early missionary was forced to examine the Mass conversions to Christianity which seems to him to have been not more than skin deep. This cosmetic brand of Christianity forced the early missionary to examine the motives for these conversions.

THE KOM CHRISTIAN EXPERIENCE OF EVANGELISATION

The German missionaries who settled in Fujua like their counterparts and fellow missionaries elsewhere adopted the school as the method that was to enable them gain a foothold in a village. It was for this reason that the Sacred Heart Missionaries opened the first school in Fujua. However their internment at Fernando Po following their expulsion from Cameroon was a blessing in disguise. The period of confinement in Fernando afforded them the opportunity to sow the seeds of the gospel once and for all in the hearts of those who had accompanied them in their flight. It was this group that would lead the first Christian course taking Christianity into areas which the missionaries would have taken years to reach. It is for this reason that the school in the immediate post war years did not play the part it had played in evangelisation in other parts of the world. Only with the further evangelisation of kom would the school approach play a vital role.

It is well known that the German Sacred Heart Missionaries arrived in Kumbo – Nso on the 31st December 1912. A few months later, in July 1913, they arrived Kom after several hours of trekking. Fon Ngam, the Fon of Kom at the time, received them and gave them a plot of land in Fujua, on the road to Laikom, about one kilometre from the present Church site at Fundong[16]

This first group of Missionaries that arrived in July 1913 was composed of Father Mannersdorfer and two Reverend Brothers in the persons of Brother Gabriel and Brother Felix Lennartz, Other accounts mention two other members of the group but it would seem that these came a few months later. They were Father Bintner, Father Foxius and Father Emonts. Fr. Baumeister later joined them. Their coming meant that other places could be visited. Thus, Mission stations were opened at Wum and Babaji from Fujua while Brother

Lennartz was in charge of building and Brother Gabriel was a kind of jack-of-all-trades doing odd jobs around the Mission. Father Mannersdorfer began a school. The predominant emphasis in his work was catechetical and linguistic. In the school, German was taught. There was an initial attempt to translate the catechism into Kom language and catechumens were enrolled into a regime lasting four years before baptism. Baptism could be administered exceptionally only in danger of death.

When the First World War broke out the German Missionaries were forced to leave. This partly explains why the Fujua Mission did not last long. No Christians had been baptised. Such a baptism might have ensured a permanent presence at the Fujua site. Matters were not helped by the fact that the vast majority of the catechumens who were being formed were forced into the German army and later interned at Fernando Po, the present Equatorial Guinea. The Fujua Mission station was thus abandoned and became a big bush with tall grass and trees. The fate that had befallen the nascent Church at Fujua was not new. It was as a result of what the Church had early warned against, a colonial administration and missionaries from the same country coming and going simultaneously. The Catholic Church is not an intruder in any country; nor is she alien to any people. It is only right, then, that those who exercise her sacred ministry should come from every nation, so that their compatriots can look to them for instruction in the law of God and leadership on the way to salvation. Wherever the local clergy exist in sufficient numbers, and are suitably trained and worthy of their holy vocation, there you can justly assume that the work of the missionary has been successful and that the Church has laid her foundations well. And if, after these foundations have been laid and these roots sunk, a persecution should be raised to dislodge her, there need be no reason to fear that she could not withstand the blow.[17] The mission in Kom was fortunate to have had one of its missionaries who were not from the colonising country. The period of colonial rule was too short and even shorter for the Church, to have sufficed for the formation of Christians, not even to talk of formation of native clergy.

Chapter Three: Motives and Methods

THE POST WAR ERA

In 1919, most of the recruited soldiers from Kom were repatriated from Fernando Po. They numbered 400 ex-soldiers, about 170 women, 50 children and 95 servants. The return of the Christian recruits to Kom was a cause for concern for the newly established colonial government, because of the religious enthusiasm of the ex-soldiers and because of their apparent loyalty to Germany. Local officials noted the tense anticipation and excitement that accompanied the soldiers' return to Kom, and advised the Resident in Buea to keep close watch on the activities of the converts. Their potential threat to the authority of the traditional rulers was not a welcome prospect to the British.

For lack of an ordained missionary in Njinikom, the Kom Christians operated virtually independently of official Church guidance. In the resulting vacuum, Michael Timneng developed a strong leadership position: he was the only Kom Christian who could read and write, and had little left to lose in terms of his relationship with traditional authorities. Father Baumeister who had himself worked in Fujua prior to his deportation baptised many of the Kom people interned at Fernando Po and urged them to return home and keep the faith alive. It would seem that many of those baptised were from Njinikom. Definitely, their leader Michael Tim was. Thus when they returned to Kom, they did not settled in Fujua some 20 kilometres off, but settled at home in Njinikom and organised a Christian community there. This was in July 1919.

Of all the Fathers who had to leave, Father Bintner who was not German but came from Luxembourg was the only one allowed to return. Coming back in 1921, he found an active Christian community in Njinikom and was determined to confirm their faith. Despite the pressure from Fon Ngam who was annoyed that the Church at Njinikom had been established without his permission, and who was further incensed by the fact that his wives were escaping to Njinikom to receive baptism, it now became increasingly clear that there would be no return to Fujua. Later in 1921, Fon Ngam instigated the removal of Michael Tim as catechist of Njinikom. The religious authorities accepted the removal hoping thereby to pacify Fon Ngam but the Church stayed at Njinikom. Fon Ngam, however, made a last ditch effort to have the Church transferred to its original site at Fujua. This was in 1922. He threatened to destroy the Church at Njinikom. Mgr. Plissonneau, the Prefect Apostolic of Adamawa, of which Njinikom (and the whole Bamenda Grasslands) was a part, who was visiting Njinikom at the time, decided to close the Church temporarily. The idea was for tempers to cool down so that a peaceful atmosphere might return. But this was not to be as Fon Ngam immediately followed up this action by arresting 12 Christians and imprisoning them in his palace.

The Njinikom Christians requested the appointment of a European priest to guide them, but this request was not granted. Occasionally, Njinikom was visited by priests from nearby Nso, where the Kom converts went for confession, and where, for example, the entire Christian community from Njinikom celebrated Christmas in 1920.

Early in 1921, Father William Bintner, a priest from Luxemburg who had previously played a role in the establishment of the German Catholic mission at Fujua, journeyed to Kom in order to persuade the Fon to allow the Christians in Njinikom to build a Church there.

After some debate, during which the Fon tried to convince Father Bintner to build the mission at Fujua, the Fon was indeed persuaded to allow the building of a Church at Njinikom, but his enthusiasm for the plan was minimal: Nonetheless, the Fon's permission to build was acquired, and a suitable location was determined. The Fon agreed that a number of villages would assist in the building of the Njinikom Church, and would provide labour and building materials. Njinikom village was to build the Church itself, while Fanantui and Babang were to build the catechist's house and the guest houses. Thus, the building enterprise involved a group of people far larger than the Christian community alone. Father Bintner was present to supervise the building and to provide spiritual guidance for the Christians, who attended Mass and doctrine classes every morning before going out to work on the building project[18].

After the Church was completed, the Catholic community grew rapidly: in the eyes of the Kom people, a Church building conferred considerable prestige on the prayer-meetings. It was not long before the Church proved too small to harbour all the Christians in Njinikom, so that catechist Michael Timneng preached outdoors in front of the Church, rather than inside the new building. By 1922, some 500 Christians were attending Njinikom chapel [19]

TRADITIONAL AUTHORITIES AND CHRISTIANITY IN CONFLICT

Not long after the Church building was erected, tension between the Fon and the Christian community came to a head when one of the Fon's wives left the palace to stay at Njinikom with fellow converts. The story of the woman, named Biwa'a, occupies a prominent place in virtually all accounts of the history of the Catholic Church in Njinikom. She was the first in a long and increasing flow of royal wives who left the palace and converted to Christianity. Their refusal to submit to the Fon's authority incensed him and troubled both colonial and Church officials throughout the period of missionary activity in Kom. Before she left the palace, Bertha Biwa'a had been secretly attending doctrine classes in Njinikom during visits to her family there. When she decided to stay in Njinikom, the Fon could not accept such an open affront to his authority.[20]

The most volatile area of conflict, not only in the early years of the mission at Njinikom, but throughout its history, was surely the competition between Church and traditional authorities for the control over women. The mission had a clear interest in converting as many women as possible, so that Christian families could be formed. It did not take Njinikom women long to discover that the Church offered them hitherto unheard-of opportunities to escape unsatisfactory marriages or family relationships. At the mission compound, they were offered some amount of physical protection and a livelihood relatively independent from their families, while they took part in the catechumen training. The power struggle was most blatantly illustrated when the wives of the Fon ran away to the mission.

It is impossible to tell whether the flight of the women to the mission was motivated by a spiritual longing to convert to Christianity, or whether their conversion to Christianity was motivated by other perceived benefits. No doubt various factors were important. Whatever the case may be, the mission's policy towards the runaway women acutely undermined the power that men in Njinikom had traditionally had over their women, and the fact that wives and unmarried daughters were granted refuge by the Church served to fuel hostilities between converts and non-Christians tremendously.

D.O. Hunt summed up the situation in Kom in 1922 as follows: The return of the Catholic Mission to Kumbo with its emotional appeal has attracted many young women to the Churches, and unfortunately for peace, wives of chiefs have been among them. In particular this has been the case with the chief of (...) Bikom, a man of between 50 and 60 with at least 100 wives of whom some are under 20. Some of these, mostly young, have left him to attend the mission Church and refused to return to him unless he gives them facilities for conversion, of which he will not hear. The result is a bitter estrangement between him and the Christian congregation, of whom some have harboured and more than harboured the runaways, so that he has practically cut off communication with the Njinikom quarter where the Church is (...) many young women fled the palace to escape the harsh treatment to which they were subjected by the older wives. According to her daughter, Bertha Biwa'a was not the Fon's wife, but a princess living at the palace. She had been made a Fon's wife by the older wives in the palace, as a form of punishment after she had run away to Njinikom and been dragged back the first time[21]:

Perpetual and violent conflict notwithstanding, the Christian community at Njinikom had grown steadily during Ngam's reign: the Catholic population of Kom numbered two thousand at the time of Fon Ngam's death[22]. The desire to practise the Christian faith was but one of many motives which contributed to the growth of the Christian community. Conversion was prompted by the wish to be modern and innovative, by the belief that Christians enjoyed supernatural protection, by the advantages attributed to education in the Whiteman's ways, and not least by the prospect of social mobility and economic gain. Christian converts from all over Kom settled at Njinikom, where they could lead lifestyles unacceptable in their home communities. Relatively free from traditional social control, they developed a community renowned for its liberal lifestyle, its monogamy, and, in time, its high level of education: "people realised that the white man's religion could liberate them from the royal yoke and they poured into Njinikom." In Njinikom, it was said, "everybody was free. Religion had liberated everybody. Women were free to do as they wished as long as they respected their husbands.[23]

It became stylish to become a Christian: "It (Christianity) was something new, and Kom people like innovation. The prayers were taught in German and it was fashionable to speak the white man's language[24]." The art of writing was regarded as white man's magic, perhaps more powerful than sorcery. Rumour had it that only Christians were protected against the Fon's chindas, so that some settled in Njinikom to enjoy protection. Many believed that Christians had access to supernatural powers which in case of emergency might prove stronger than those connected to traditional beliefs[25].

Educational opportunities attracted a great number of converts to Njinikom. Initially the schooling offered consisted of doctrine classes and basic literacy at a so-called hedge-school. Later, when the school was granted European leadership, Njinikom became known as the educational centre for Kom. The colonial administration was sceptical about the motives for conversion to Christianity. In 1922, the D.O. claimed that runaway wives who sought refuge at the mission compound were merely trying to "avoid their obligations to their husbands or parents."

The colonial Administrator was convinced beyond doubt that the conversions were not genuine. He saw the early conversions simply as one of those fascinations, which Africans were running after. He went on to say "Religion, like anything else takes a hold on the native, is an innovation, and has a fascination for them but they should remember that the path to Christianity is encompassed with tribulation and sorrow and until civilisation makes more progress among them, their lot will not be an easy one." He did not immediately see that the tribulations and sorrows were the daily lot of some Christians already. The other side of the coin alluded to by the colonial report was that converts relinquished to a large degree their position within traditional society. The price they paid for the perceived benefits of Christianity often amounted to ostracisation. Former networks providing social and emotional security frequently ceased to function as such when someone chose to affiliate with the new religion. The dependence of the converts on the Church community was, by consequence, far-reaching. The root causes that urge the pagans here to become Christians have given food for thought[26].

Njinikom owing to the presence of the Church had become one of the centres and stronghold of early Christianity not just in kom but even beyond. All over kom land and even beyond people seeking to become Christians were gradually gravitating and drifting towards Njinikom. In and out of kom itself a good number of the early converts to Christianity seem to have been women and women remain in some cases the centre of controversy and bone of contention between the Catholic Church and the traditional authority. A good number of these women seemed to have been escaping from a forced marriage. Examples abound in and out of kom. During this trouble there was a girl of ten years whom the parents had given the old chief according to their native customs by the name of Ngum. She came to doctrine classes and the parents were trying to stop her but were unable to do it. Then they informed the chief that the wife had joined the Catholic Christians ... on the next day she was led along the road to kom. On the following day the chief sent three of his big men to Njinikom to force her back to Bafut. They went first to the chief of Bikom and the chief told them to go and search in Njinikom.[27] The issue of infant marriages and runaway wives seeking refuge in the missions was a widespread problem. In many instances "the mission acts like a kind of marriage market and refuge for wives who wish to leave their husbands, against Native laws and Custom. This in itself naturally makes the mission unpopular among the chiefs as each of these marriages has been made in direct opposition to the wishes of the lawful guardian of the women" [28]

It is important to examine the underlining motives for these conversions to Christianity in face of opposition from traditional authorities. The early missionaries preached about a God who was merciful and rewards people according to their deeds in the world to come. Secondly, for Christians to come to know him and to enjoy the fruits of eternal life they would have to reject and denounce all practices that were considered satanic and demonic in origin such as witchcraft and bad medicines. These made some sense to the people who were living in the clutches of wizards and at the mercy of witchdoctors. Naturally at the time when life expectancy was low and infant mortality high people often saw deaths from natural causes as a result of witchcraft and thus the promise of the protection Christianity could offer was appealing to many who were looking for answers.

Salvation which Christianity could offer in this life by protecting them from the malevolent actions of witches and wizards reached its final fulfilment in heaven. For those who faithfully lived Christian lives their reward was great in heaven where God with his angels lived in glory. As results of the appealing message of Christianity, people began to flock to Christianity abandoning their former practices, charms, bad medicines and seeking refuge in the Church. Material benefits no doubt attracted some Christians who saw the religion of the Whiteman as a way forward in the new dispensation.

On June 16 1926, Fon Ngam died without having resolved many issues with the church. Conflict over the burial of Nafoin Naya'a fuinkun had strained relations with the church. Ndi Kuoh, Fon Ngam's Parallel cousin succeeded him on the throne. He adopted a reconciliatory approach and succeeded in healing the rift with his estranged Christian subjects by permitting the churches to reopen in other three populous areas of Kom for a probationary period of six months. He succeeded in handling the removal and reburial of Naya'a Funkuin. By the end of 1926, the atmosphere was peaceful enough to allow for the creation of a Parish in Njinikom. On March 29 1927, Njinikom became a Parish. This was almost a year following the death of Fon Ngam.

FURTHER EXPANSION OF CHRISTIANITY IN KOM

After the creation of Njinikom Parish in 1927, Fundong was ignored for a time. It was not exactly on the trek route of the Fathers. It was grazing ground for cattle. Rather it is Achain that was visited by the Missionaries in their long treks.

The present mission in Fundong was acquired in the early 1940s. it was given by the Fon who asked the Quarter Head of Atoini to allocate land for the Church. Bobe Ketchah, the Quarter Head, showed the present site since he wanted the whole area. It is important to note that the expansion of the Catholic Church in the areas out of Njinikom heavily depended on Christians who had come over from Njinikom. Although these Christians were not missionaries in the real sense of the word, they gradually took on the role of missionaries. Many of them were Christians who had come over from Njinikom to succeed the compounds of their uncles. It was these fall away Christians who provided both the nucleus and personnel for the early Christian communities in the areas out of Njinikom. Njinikom had received Christianity and sustained it virtually during the priestless period following the defeat of the Germans and the subsequent expulsion of the Sacred Heart Missionaries, through the ex-soldiers. The areas out of Njinikom would receive Christianity mainly through Christians who had come over from Njinikom. The early missionaries relied heavily on these recovering Christians. Although traditional authorities of the kom palace had been a stumbling block and confrontations between the palace and the Church were a common feature, the early priests saw the Quarter Heads' compounds as a gateway to the evangelisation of the area. It was precisely so because following the death of Fon Ngam, his successor Fon Ndi ushered in the détente.

INDIGENOUS MISSIONARY INITIATIVES

Providentially, the Catholics would seem to have been helped in their efforts to establish at Fundong by an individual called Anyway Ndichia. As a private citizen returning from the 'Coast', i.e. from the Littoral and South West areas of Cameroon and having seen what was happening there and being enlightened by it, he opened a school next to the Mission plot in 1946. In 1949, the Mission took over the school and incorporated it into the Mission. This was the beginning of the Catholic mission.

Another founding Member of the Church in Fundong was Bobe Kain. He started his missionary work at Benakma .During his stay at this mission station many people were converted to become Catholic Christians. During this time all the catechists paid regular visits to Kumbo to keep in touch with the Parish there as well the first Friday of every month devotions. Bobe Kain worked as a catechist in Bafmeng as well as Mbongkisu. Following the death of his uncle in 1950 he was forced to move to Fundong. From 1950 – 1954 He remained a key person in the work of evangelisation. He was help by another Christian Peter Diang.

An important date during this period is January 1954, when Peter Diang Ketchah was sent out to Fundong. Being one of the first Christians of the Parish, he was sent to Fundong by Father Woodman, after completing his standard six at Njinikom. He kept

Chapter Three: Motives and Methods

Anyway Ndichia and Peter Ndiang

the Mission going, teaching doctrine and conducting services on Sundays. So persuasive was his influence that he was referred to as 'Father' Diang. He was soon joined by a band of other Christians who had had contact with the Njinikom Christian community.

With all these Christians coming forward and willing to live out their Christian commitment, Father Francis Woodman saw the big possibilities for evangelization if parishes were opened in Fundong to cater for the Areas out of Njinikom and in Ashing to look after the Belo Valley. Accordingly, in 1964 he asked Bishop Jules Peeters if these places could not be opened up as 'Head-Missions', that is, as parishes. Due to a lack of Priests, the Bishop could not reply positively to this request even after it was repeated in 1967. But four years later this wish became a reality.

As already stated, in 1964, Father Woodman wrote from Njinikom asking that Fundong be made a Parish. This request was repeated in 1967. The prayers of Father Woodman were answered on the 21st November 1971, the Feast of Christ the King, the day on which Fundong became a Parish. It was one of the first Parishes to be created after the coming into being of Bamenda Archdiocese. Father Joseph Holzhneckt who was at the time the Parish Priest at Njinikom was named the first Parish Priest.

The individual missionary had given up his country and his family in order to aid the extension of the faith. When he sets out on his long and often dangerous journey he is, as a rule, eager and ready to brave the most gruelling hardships, and all he asks is an opportunity to win for Christ as many souls as possible. Furthermore, the superior of a mission should make it one of his primary concerns to expand and fully develop his mission. The entire region within the boundaries of his mission has been committed to his care. Consequently, he must work for the eternal salvation of every person living there. If, out of an immense populace, he has converted a few thousand people, he has no reason to lapse into complacency. He must become a guide and a protector for these children he has brought forth in Jesus Christ; he must see to their spiritual nourishment and he must not let a single one of them slip away and perish. But he must do more than this. He must not consider that he is properly discharging the duties of his office unless he is working constantly and with all the vigour he can muster to bring the other, far more numerous, inhabitants of the area to partake of the Christian truth and the Christian life[29] With these words in mind Njinikom thus became the launching pad and springboard for the missionaries.

MISSIONARY TACTICS AND MANOEUVRES

The Mill Hill missionaries adopted a policy of grouping their priests together and not scattering them all over the mission area. It was from one mission that the Missionaries embarked on routine treks to the mission stations and explored territories. The Treks towards the other areas of kom out of Njinikom usually started on Saturday, it was the same for Njinikijem treks, as well as treks from Njinikom to Mmen. The Treks were organised in such a way that Sunday always met the priest in the big outstations where the priest celebrated the Eucharist.

Routine treks to mission Stations were constant features of this early period. The priest going on mission station visitation employed the services of the carriers who were often Christians from Njinikom and whose payment at times was the marking of the Christian contribution cards. This group of carriers formed the congregation and assisted the priest at Mass in explaining the word to the people as well as directing the priest in areas where it was impossible for the priest to proceed without their aid.

The routine treks were undertaken by all the priests who took turns when there were more than two priests in the parish. These treks lasted for a period of one to two weeks and even beyond. In the case of Njinikom Parish treks sometimes took close to a month at the time when Njinikom was second only to Shisong and its area of jurisdiction covered the territory of the present day Bamenda Archdiocese. These Treks were guided by a trek book which was an exercise book indicating the area covered and pastoral problems encountered in the stations. This was an important asset for the priest who avoided the problem of one Christian playing one priest against another, keeping the priest well informed of the activities of the missions and the nature of the mission in question. The priest regularly discussed the problems encountered and mapped out the way forward in the missions and the mission to be undertaken. The itinerary of the priest was well known to the Christians.

Everywhere the priest went they were opened to the needs of the people. The listened to their worries, engaged them in frank discussions. For those who were already Christians, visible and important signs of Catholicism like medals and other sacramentals were offered. Above all the priest remained very close to the people in time of need. Priests went as far as Achain and Njinikijem on foot to administer the sacrament of the sick. While looking further afield the gains at home were consolidated through on going catechesis. This was done weekly following a well thought out program along age groups from Monday to Friday.

The chain of command was well mapped out the roles among the priests were carefully shared out. The Parish Priest was at the helm of the Parish and represented the parish before the traditional and civil authorities. From this vantage point the Parish priest coordinated the missionary moves and consolidated what was already gained.

Material gifts were given out to needy Christians to assists them one way or the other. The priests assisted some Christians to undergo training in professional schools such as the Teachers Training College and the school of nursing. Material gifts such as clothes, shoes, were given out to needy persons. Some of the people who were sent to training colleges in many cases became very useful to the Church. On completion of school, some the past pupils of standard six who had shown an interest in gaining admission into the Teachers Training College Bambui and Bojongo were employed as catechists. This was an attractive strategy because many of them had first hand knowledge of the Simple English Catechism which was the standard text book in use in schools at the time. Besides their knowledge in the field of Christian religion they were indigenes armed with the language of the people. Many of them were the catechist and the teacher at the same time. Knowing that the school was the main gateway and possible means of gaining a foothold in many villages and owing to the shortage of personnel the option of using standard six pupils was plausible.

The early missionaries in Njinikom were lucky to have been spared the trouble of starting the missions in kom in general. The nucleus laid by the departing Sacred Heart Missionaries remained the foundation on which the Mill Hill missionaries were later to build.

However it was incumbent on them to go into unexplored areas to establish new missions or rekindle the faith in fall away Christians. It was almost a nightmare in some cases for the priest to visit certain territories where hostilities could easily erupt. The early missionaries in some cases came close to some of the dark mysterious realities of the African spiritual world. One of these to be missions was Aduk. The Priest was going there for the first time. No priest had ever stayed in the village. The first visit of the Priest to Aduk was very eventful. The Church compound housed the juju. Some years earlier another missionary had shared the same experience in the Ibo land. Bishop Shanahan had to live in a thatched hut which up to that time had been the shrine of a pagan idol. Shanahan stayed some days with them in the hut, where they shared their living quarters with the juju, an unnerving concoction of wooden beams, creepers, feathers and scraps of cloths[30]

During their first visit to Aduk the priest and his travelling companion came straight to the Quarter Head's compound. He was not at home and they saw nobody except little children. They sat down on stones on the veranda of different houses to rest....In this compound of the Quarter Head there was a village 'juju' (mask) called "Mbeng" meaning Rain 'juju.' A shrine of "Mbeng" stood right in the middle of the courtyard of the compound with stones neatly built round it for people to sit on. Every morning, nursing mothers of the compound sat on some of the stones to wash their babies. Any nursing woman sat on the stone facing her house to wash her child and rub the child with cam wood or palm oil. It was held in the village that only initiated members of "Mbeng" could sit on those stones, and children of the compound too. Sometimes when there was an assembly of the villagers in that compound, ordinary villagers were given the privilege to sit on them.[31]

Missionaries going into unexplored areas for the first time had hardly been spared the ordeal of rejection of their offer. There were villages Shanahan in his own days could sense the presence of evil as soon as he entered. There were villages which he was physically unable to enter. His offers of school were contemptuously rejected. It was to be the same case at Aduk in the compound of the juju.[32] Here was a repeat of almost a similar scenario. The Quarter Head returned late at night. The Priest met him and told him the purpose of his visit to the village. "I want to open a Catholic school and a Catholic Church too in your village. Could you allocate a piece of land for that?" The Quarter Head replied, "No, I have land only for women to farm. No plot for Church and school." The priest felt quite defeated and walked out of the house in disgust.[33]

The priest going on mission visitation or looking for unexplored areas often took along people who acted as carriers and guides and formed the congregation for the liturgical celebration wherever he went. These carriers assisted not only in carrying the physical goods or also facilitated the transmission of the spiritual goods. The carriers who were often Christians themselves assisted the priests in explaining the sacred mysteries to the people. Still in Aduk it is important to see how the prevailing mentality about white priests prevented the missionaries from reaching the people. It was often a mentality coloured by superstition based on their beliefs in African Traditional Religion. The next morning Mass was celebrated in the small poky house where he spent the night. It was a small dark house of two beds only. The women of the compound together with their children gathered at the door to watch what was going on in the house. The mother of the boy in whose house Mass was being celebrated kept crying outside that her son's house was being defiled. After Mass and breakfast, they left for Achain where they stayed the night and celebrated Holy Mass the next morning, left for Abuh via a forest full of nettles to Muteff and Abuh. To walk through that forest was like walking through fire or through a field of wild bees escaping from a hive.[34]

In most cases when the early missionaries set out to evangelise in the 1960's there was no Church house in most of the villages since they were still trying to establish Christian faith. In those days' treks were for primary evangelisation. The routine treks covered in some cases a period of a month. The treks were guided by the Trek book which was an exercise book indicating the problems or difficulties encountered in the stations. At these places the priest usually celebrated Mass in the Quarter Head's compound where he was accommodated. He celebrated Mass in the open air in the courtyard where everybody in the compound could see. There were no catechists in these places. Thus the compounds of the Quarter Heads became a gateway for the priest to gain entrance and maintain a suitable foothold in the villages where he was welcomed. It seemed that no direct attempt was made in most cases to convert these Quarter Heads themselves. During the preliminary visits the priest spent most of his time talking to the Quarter Heads or village Heads explaining the purpose of his visit and what Catholic faith was all about when he was about to leave he often entrusted the mission to any Christian he found around to enlighten the Quarter Heads and the others. It was in some cases very frustrating.

Some of the Quarter Heads were very apprehensive about Christianity. Many harboured misgivings surrounded by fear about the Christian faith. For example, when the early missionary came to Ngwa, the Quarter Head denied the priest permission to enter his compound. He claimed that there had been no notification from the Father about the visit to his compound and quarter. Because of this, he would not allow him to stay in his compound. The Father explained to him that he had earlier sent information to the Quarter Head through a schoolteacher from Achain to bring to him. The Quarter Head was not yet convinced. He was not really after the notification letter from the priest, but was afraid of the priest because of the many weird stories he had heard about Reverend Fathers. How they can curse one to go mad and can destroy bad medicines in people's compounds. The Father also went about with the seven books of Moses and read them daily. The Quarter Head said; Father if I allow you to lodge in my compound, you will destroy it and also destroy my village. Go back to that your Njinikom. I have no place to house you and all these people.[35] This was precisely so because at the entrance of the compound lay a ritual stone where seasonal ritualistic ceremonies were carried out to initiate the planting season and also to protect crops from being destroyed by "people travelling in the wind."

The carriers who went along with the priests, in many ways proved more useful than carriers. In many cases, though banking their hopes on the colonial administration or the government, they came to the aid of the early missionaries often surmounting obstacles which otherwise would have made it impossible for the priests to proceed. In one instance at Ngwa, Pa Alex, a Christian from Njinikom confronted the Quarter Head. In the compound where the ritual stone was, he stood on the opposite side of the stone facing the

Quarter Head, who said that he, Pa Alex would first enter and all the others would enter after him, like a masked "juju"; backward. He turned himself and gave his back to the Quarter Head and walked across the ritual stone into the compound. He then ordered all the carriers of the Father to follow him and they did. They got into the courtyard and Pa Alex asked the Quarter Head to bring a chair for the Rev. Father to sit on. He called to the Quarter Head. "Bonteh" "if this Whiteman dies in your compound you will be held responsible. You and your entire village will be held and taken to Bamenda as prisoners. Bring him chop and show a house where his cook will prepare lunch for him, also give him a house to sleep. You know white men always sleep during the day and at night when everybody will be in bed sleeping, he will be going around watching all those who walk about in different forms at night. You must count yourself lucky to have this Whiteman in your compound today."[36] With hindsight one can easily see the enormous sacrifice the early missionaries made for primary evangelisation. Braving all odds the early missionaries did all in their power to bring the good news to unevangelised areas.

African Christians regarded the Whiteman or even more so the missionaries as being above the reach of charms and bad medicines. By virtue of their colour and religion, it was believed, certain portent African concoctions were rendered impotent in the face of the white missionaries. It is for this reason that he was often regarded with suspicion. The actions of missionaries apparently to the Africans seem to have confirmed this misguided belief. Was his superiority in technology also seen to extend into the sphere of his superiority in religion? In the evening when all the boys of the village came to admire their friend's house that had the honour to accommodate a Whiteman...at the centre of the house was a hearth (fireplace) with three stones to hold the fire when it was lit. Behind the main stone there was a horn of a she goat with a cover made of cowries and a porcupine's pin stuck into the lid. It was well fitted into the ground behind the main stone. The priest got up from his seat and walked round the room and each time he came close to the horn, he stopped and looked at it. He went round the room about three times, then pulled out the horn from the ground and shook it close to his ears. He then put it back on the ground. After sometime the Father picked up the horn again and started to empty its contents. The youths told him not to attempt to open it because it contained very bad medicines. The Father gave no heed to what they were saying. He opened it and emptied its contents. Three cowries came out of the horn. The youths of the village fled leaving their friend to the fate of his generosity. The next day Mass was celebrated in the courtyard. Nobody from the compound dared to witness it. They stayed behind closed doors till it was over.[37]

The matrilineal system of succession helped in no mean way the course of Christianity in the areas outside Njinikom. The Christians who had come over from Njinikom to succeed their uncles' compounds in other areas of kom out of Njinikom proved to be very instrumental in the evangelisation process. The story of the Church at Abuh begins with a Christian couple that had come over from Njinikom to inherit an uncle's compound. This compound was home to the juju 'Niba',[38] as well as the harmless 'Chong'[39]. Mass was celebrated in the open air within the courtyard. The people of the compound stood at distance watching and making gestures and comments. It was the same case with the Church in Mboh Village. This was mainly the work of Gabriel Asang and his wife, Odilia Nange. They came from Njinikom where they themselves had received baptism and settled at Mboh at a time when the Church did not exist. It was this couple that provided the nucleus of the first Christian community. Here the Father succeeded through the aid of one Christian couple, Gabriel Asang and wife Odilia Nange who came from Njinikom and inherited an uncle's compound. Gabriel and Odilia had not been to Mass since the year they came to Mboh as far back as 1950, even though Njinikom was within their reach on foot. They were so delighted to see the Father in their village and immediately in the evening they turned up to report themselves to the Father as lost Christians. The Father admonished them of the danger they had been in and exhorted them to begin a new life again and be the first Disciples of Christ to Mboh people. They accepted admonition and the exhortation and as a sign of their gratitude, Gabriel and Odilia offered a piece of land behind their compound for the Father to build a Church. They made their confession and went to communion after ten years of silent sufferings and hungering for the Lord.[40]

The early missionaries had developed a good tactic of getting to people. The Quarter Head's compound became the first stop for a missionary when he entered a village. When a missionary got a plot to build a Church, a catechist was sent straight to the Quarter Head and he was not allowed to stay anywhere except with the Quarter Head until the Church was built and the first group of Christians were able to make their presence felt in the village. In this wise, he got a good grip of the Quarter Head and his villagers. In every out station the priests visited, Priests taught doctrine to the Christians in the evening before evening prayers and confessions. Where there were no Christians yet, he took the catechumens and tested them from one question to the other and cursing them at the same time when they could not answer.

At Elemiwong the Father founded a Church in the compound of the Quarter Head, Papa Bartholomew, a Catholic who came from Wombong to succeed a compound there. He was still a faithful Catholic at heart though he inherited so many wives. He never failed to pray his Rosary and evening prayers from his German prayer book. It was very easy to establish in a village where they could find some lapsed Christians who came had come to inherit an uncle's compound. Through their cooperation and influence the Father received no opposition. They were of tremendous help to establish the faith in such villages. Very often most of them offered their farms to build the first Church in the village.

All over the region was the presence of the ex-German soldiers who had become Christians. Unlike in Njinikom the Christians here often were persecuted. The seeds for a Mission Station at Djichami were sown as far back as the early 1920s, following the return of Christians from Fernando Po. The pioneer group of Christians were later to suffer persecution from the hands of Ayeah Ngoin, heir to the throne of kom. He did everything to frustrate the efforts at setting up a Christian community at Belo. Persecutions began when they gathered material for the construction of the Church. With the assistance of thugs, the early group of Christians were forced to carry the bamboos right to the Acha River. However, the group of Christians mustered courage, regrouped and acquired a piece of land where in 1921, they constructed a Church house at Njinikijem[41].

Following the example of the pioneer group from Njinikijem, the group of Christians from Djichami who had returned from Fernando Po, started a prayer group. For fear of more persecutions they called it a dance group which held once a week. All songs sang were hymns and psalms. Each dance session ended with a short prayer. There was little doctrine taught. In 1939 a dynamic member joined the group and became the first catechist. He was gifted at composing songs, hymns and had a bugle which attracted more members[42]. The scenario of Christians hiding under the cloak of a dance group to pray was not uncommon. Out of Njinikom, many areas made use of this tactic. The wrath of traditional rulers was feared so much so that no group tried to profess their faith in public.

The early missionaries employed the use of local languages in teaching doctrine, conducting prayers and singing in Church and interpretation of the homily in the local language on Sunday by the catechist. Among the attainments necessary for the life of a missionary, a place of paramount importance must obviously be granted to the language of the people to whose salvation he will devote himself. He should not be content with a smattering of the language, but should be able to speak it readily and competently. For in this respect he is under an obligation to all those he deals with, the learned and the ignorant alike, and he will soon realize the advantage a command of their language gives him in the task of winning the confidence of the populace. If he is earnest about his work, he will be particularly reluctant to delegate the explanation of Christian doctrine to his catechists. He will insist upon reserving this duty to himself. Since he has been sent to the missions for no other purpose, after all, than to preach the gospel, he will even come to look on these instruction periods as the most important part of his work. There will also be occasions when, in his position as representative and interpreter of our holy Faith, he will have to associate with the dignitaries of the district. Or he may be invited to appear at scholarly gatherings. How will he maintain his dignity under these circumstances if he cannot make himself understood because he does not know the language?[43]

It seems that the use of local languages was gradually abandoned after 1950. Gradually, it was argued that, since no one local language could be used all over West Cameroon, the use of local languages in the Liturgy was a bad thing This consensus in favour of the use of local languages, at least as far as Catechetics are concerned, is really a return to the policy of the early Fathers of this Diocese. When Father Moran arrived at Shisong in May 1923, the policy of using the local language followed by earlier missionaries was dropped and Pidgin English was adopted. By the end of the 'twenties, the utter inadequacy and inefficacy of Pidgin English for Catechetics in these grasslands became evident for all to see. Consequently, Mgr. Rogan demanded a change of policy. It was thus that translations of the Catechism and of Prayers and numberless popular devotions were undertaken in Lamnso, Kom, Kijerm, Limbum, Mankon, and other languages in the Bamenda Grasslands. We must salute the work of those Fathers and Catechists who undertook these translations. It is a fact that the Catholic Faith would never have made the progress it made in these Grasslands in the nineteen thirties and forties were it not for that change in policy[44].

Between 1931 and 1949, there was a very consistent policy concerning local languages. The importance of Catechetics in the local language was frequently stressed, and it was also stipulated that every Father should endeavour to master at least one local language. Perhaps not many Fathers achieved this, but the Catechisms and Prayers in the local languages certainly achieved something as regards acculturation.

One thing is certain: a study of the Minutes of the Provincial (or Vicariate) Meetings of the Mill Hill Fathers in the nineteen thirties and forties reveals that they were constantly aware of the fact that even though Pidgin might prove handy in talking to people, it was inadequate as an instrument for reaching the souls of the people; hence the insistence on the necessity for the learning of at least one local language. The first German Fathers at Shisong were confronted with this problem. I have it on good authority that Mgr. Plissonneau, author of the Pidgin English Catechism that was adopted in Prefecture Apostolic of Buea, admitted himself, in his last Report to Rome that he recognised the inevitable superficiality that would result if local languages were not adopted for Evangelisation.[45]

Some of the practices applied by the early missionaries may seem shocking, judging with the mentality of today. One of these methods applied was public punishment and this did not rule out corporal punishment. Public sanctions were imposed on defaulters both men and women alike. They were required to work in the mission compound for weeks and even months in some cases before they were allowed to receive the sacrament of reconciliation. In some cases it went beyond manual work. Some of the missionaries blatantly violated prevailing guidelines for missionary conduct. Like his model, the Lord Jesus, the good missionary burns with charity, and he numbers even the most abandoned unbelievers among God's children, redeemed like everyone else with the ransom of the divine blood. Their lowly difference does not exasperate him; their immorality does not dishearten him. His bearing toward them is neither scornful nor fastidious; his treatment of them is neither harsh nor rough. Instead, he makes use of all the arts of Christian kindness to attract them to himself, so that he may eventually lead them into the arms of Christ, into the embrace of the Good Shepherd. He makes it a custom to ponder the thought expressed in Holy Scripture[46]. Corporal punishment was not totally ruled out as a sanction in the missions. It was a matter of public knowledge that the officials of the Catholic mission, both European and Africans, made a regular practice of inflicting corporal punishment on their followers for any moral lapse or lack of discipline so long as these punishments occasioned no harm and were inflicted with the consent of those punished[47].

By and large, the task of the early missionaries was a daunting one, fraught with all kinds of difficulties on almost every front. It was a venture whose success was apparently very precarious. The zeal of these early missionaries was aided by the presence of the colonial authorities. However, in the end it was up to the Africans themselves to accept or reject the word, following the expulsion of the Germans from Cameroon. The missionary policy of using education as bait paid off to some extent but it made the Church look like an affaire of the educated. Apart from the Christians interned at Fernando who received some education while there and those around them, Christianity seemed to have been an affair for the educated. In some cases, those out of regular schooling were sometimes cut out of the regular milieu of Christian evangelisation.

A school built on school children may not always bear the expected fruits in relation to the general population. It was important to note the mentality of Africans regarding education at the out set. Those who went to school were usually the very stubborn children or children whose feet were infested with jiggers. The school was considered by the villagers as punishment ground. It used to be said that if you did not behave well, your Father would send you to school. Even in school some parents objected to the children becoming Christians[48]. Schools were actually nurseries for the new Church in many African countries. This insertion of the Church in the society through the school was bound to have dangerous consequences. It failed to address the needs of adult's right from its inception which may have been at odds with Christianity.

It is important to examine and critically evaluate with hindsight the results of these approaches of evangelisation and what lessons one can learn from them. The same also applies to the motives of conversion to Christianity the world over and in African in particular and what consequences that has had for Christianity today in Africa. What pastoral steps can be taken to prepare for a new generation of Christians? All over Africa today the hangover of these approaches applied virtually wholesale in many areas continue to haunt the church in the mentality prevailing in the Church today.

Notes

1. John Paul II, (1990) Encyclical Letter, Redemptoris Missio, on the Mission of the Redeemer, Vatican

2. Letter to Diognetus on the life style of Christians 2nd century in Jurgens William, (1992) The Faith of Our Fathers Volume one Theological publications in India.

3. Bill R Austin(1983) Austin's Topical history of Christianity, Tyndale Publishers, Inc pg. 95

4. Letter 93;16f of 408; wholesome coercion in Jurgens William, (1992) The Faith of Our Fathers Volume one Theological publications in India.

5. St. Augustine's Letter 185:11.24 of 417, on Luke 14:23"Compel them to come in!" in Jurgens William, (1992) The Faith of Our Fathers Volume one Theological publications in India.

6. Schaff,Philip History of the Christian Church, Volume IV: Mediaeval Christianity. A.D. 590-1073.

7. Ibid.

8. Bill R op. cit., p.159.

9. Carol Koch (1994) The Catholic Church, journey wisdom and mission. St. Mary's Press pg 223.
10. Pope Alexander, (1493) Papal Bull VI Inter Caetera.
11. Pope Pius XI (1926) Rerum Ecclesiae On Catholic mission no. 6.
12. Thomas Kiggins (1991)Maynooth Mission to Africa, The Story of St. Patrick's Kiltegan. Gill and MacMillan.
13. Comby Jean () How to read Church History Volume I from the beginning to the fifteenth century.
14. Forristal Desmod (1990). The Second Burial of Bishop Shanahan, Dublin,Veritas Publication.
15. Ibid.
16. The Baptists have since settle at the site of this first Mission at Fujua and have a Church and a school there.
17. Benedict XV. Op. cit.
18. De Vries Jacqueline op. cit.
19. Ibid.
20. Ibid.
21. De Vries op. cit.
22. Boh, Gregory,1987) an address presented by the President of the Njinikom Parish Council on the Occasion of the Diamond Jubilee of the Founding of St. Anthony's Parish (1927-1987) Njinikom in De Vries Jacqueline (1998) Catholic Mission, Colonial government and Indigenous Response in Kom (Cameroon) African studies centre.
23. De Vries op. cit.
24. Ndi 1986 op. cit.
25. De Vries cited op.
26. Ibid
27. The story of Angela Ngum in O'Neil Robert(1995) Mission to the Southern Cameroons, Burns and Oates.
28. Extract, 1930 Report 11/6/30,BA sd/1920/2. in De Vries Jacqueline (1998) Catholic Mission, Colonial government and Indigenous Response in Kom (Cameroon) African studies centre.

29. Ibid no.11.
30. Bulletin de la congregation, XXV, P 370 in Forristal Desmond, (1990) The second Burial of Bishop Shanahan, Veritas Publication.
31. John Musi Yonghabi. A Mission Boy From Nowhere to Somewhere. Copy Printing Technology Bamenda. The Missionaries whose mission is described here was Fr. John McKeogh. The author was at this time the houseboy of the Priest.
32. Ibid.
33. Ibid.
34. Ibid.
35. Ibid.
36. Ibid.
37. Ibid.
38. A traditional juju usually two in number believe to be owned only by a dumb with mystical powers.
39. John Musi Yonghabi. A Mission Boy: From Nowhere to Somewhere. Copy Printing Technology Bamenda
40. Ibid.
41. The History of the Catholic Church in Fuli Kom (2000) 1975-2000. A silver Jubilee publication. Copy Printing Technology Bamenda.
42. Ibid
43. Benedict XV cit. op. no. 24.
44. Verdzekov Paul () The Language Problem of the early German Missionaries in Nso Area in Mbuy Tatah, H.,(1995) Shepherd on the Bamenda Highland.
45. Ibid
46. Benedict XV op. cit.
47. Annet to the Registrar 16/11/28 in Ndi Anthony (2004) Mill Hill Missionaries in Southern Cameroon, Nairobi.
48. Cf Souvenir St. Gabriel's Parish Bafmeng. 1965-1990.

CHAPTER FOUR

PRESENT DAY CHALLENGES

INTRODUCTION
Besides colonialism, one of the themes that have received a bad press from prominent Cameroonian writers is Christianity. Significant numbers of writers have portrayed Christianity and specifically Catholicism in often derogatory and pejorative terms. Some novels present colonialism together with Christianity as a collapsing enterprise. Prominent among these writers are Mongo Beti, Kenjo Jumbam, and Ferdinand Oyono. In some of these writings, Catholicism is attacked even in vitriolic terms. Most of these writers if not all were products of Catholic education knowing that formal and western styled education for many years was the privileged monopoly of missionary outreach. It is very unlikely that these illustrious sons of this country were not direct beneficiaries of the sweat and toil of the very missionaries who they freely portray in no friendly terms. The writings of these authors give us some food for thought. Did these scholars have an axe to grind with the early missionaries?

One negative element in the rapid expansion of mission schools in the 1950s was the lack of gentleness with which it was put into effect by many of the missionaries. A number used high-handed methods and bullying tactics in acquiring sites, exacting local contributions and dealing with Teachers (…) this less than gentle approach was not confined to educational matters or indeed to this period. However, it was exacerbated by the emergence of a more sophisticated and politicised African with whom the missionary no longer enjoyed the rapport which had been there when the former was a school boy. Faced with this new sophistication, which was often overtly European, the missionary was not unknown to respond with sarcasm and cynicism. The African would appear to have accepted any such gracelessness with great tolerance. Looking back from the more tranquil vantage point of life, many of the missionaries regret their behaviour and wish they had tempered zeal with greater respect.[1]

The hangover of such gracelessness on the part of missionaries has not completely vanished. It was not particular to European clergy or limited to Africa and remains a lesson for all missionaries at all times, be they African or European. The hangover of such gracelessness continues the haunt the Church not only in Africa but as well as in Europe, Asia and Latin America. The cases of the Aborigines in Australia and the Irish cases of abuses in Ireland are but a few cases in point. Most of the priests and brothers were men of outstanding character and dedication but there were occasional scandals hushed up at the time and still largely inaccessible to many researchers. Another temptation strengthened by the example of many colonial officials, was to treat Africans as an inferior branch of the human race. Brother Kevin mentions one of the Alsatian brothers whose ungovernable temper led to the death of two Africans[2]. In Shisong Thaddeus Taba used to beat the drum in the school barracks at night, tears streaming down his cheeks, as the boys clustered around and danced not to make merry but to drown their sorrows. For the Father in charge believed in a lavished systematic use of the cane of the whip and ruled with an iron, German sternness which to the boys amounted to a reign of terror. So at night around the drum they stumped and wept and sang:

> Eh Poto, hi-e hi-e
> Eh Poto, hi-e hi-e
> Eh Poto, hi-e hi-e
> Ah ta Poto
> Ah dzer Poto
> Ah ayen Poto- hi-e, hie.

Poto was a deliberate deformation of Pater or Father to hide the fact that they were bemoaning the rule of the priest in charge of the school. Missionary Zeal and sacrifices of the missionaries were tainted by the very gracelessness with which they carried out their mission.

SUBTLE ANTI CHRISTIAN LITERATURE AND THE PHENOMENON OF REVERSION

Kenjo Jumbam is one of those writers whose writing gives us an idea of the predicaments and dilemma faced by early missionaries, the propagators and the Africans, the recipients and beneficiaries of Christian faith in general and Catholicism in particular. The second chapter of *The white man of God* presents Christianity as an enterprise in apparent failure. After years of labouring in the Lord's vineyard, the people remain deeply rooted in the very traditions they were expected to and should have turned their backs on. In what is presented as a contest between the most powerful juju in the land and the Whiteman of God, in what can be seen almost as a proof of authenticity and vindication, the white man of God alongside his God is seen as helpless in front of the most powerful juju of the land.

Ferdinand Oyono in his novel *The Old Man and The Medal* freely satirizes the colonial situation through the eyes of an African Meka an old villager who is presented as loyal to the Whiteman. Though he satirizes colonialism, Catholicism is not left out in this satire. Catholicism is presented as an extension of colonial enterprise. The French Catholic Priest, Father Vandermayer is presented as a colonialist rather than a missionary. He is even referred to by Meka as a crook. After Meka's disgrace at the community centre, all those superstitions spring to his mind like a great tide, sweeping away the years of Christian teaching and promise[3].

These writings were part of the 'Back to Cameroonian Culture Campaign', which sought to discredit Catholicism. Reflecting on this rather disturbing trend in the flow of literature which seemingly was aimed at undermining and denigrating Christianity, the then Archbishop of Bamenda, Paul Verdzekov, went on to say that "In Francophone Cameroon, indigenous priests are in the front-line of the research that is going on in this field at various levels in the parishes, in secondary schools, at the University of Yaoundé. As regards the 'BACK TO CAMEROONIAN CULTURE CAMPAIGN' may I call our attention to the enormous amount of theses that are being written on themes around Traditional Religion by the young graduates of Yaoundé University? From what I have seen, I believe that this theme seems to be by far the most popular.

Our young people too are strongly influenced by the ideas on traditional religion and culture in the many African Novels that they read. Practically all these Novels present Christianity as foreign to Africa and as an enemy to the African's cultural heritage. Can we afford to ignore these developments? What strategy do we adopt to meet the new changes?"[4]

No Cameroonian novelist presents Christianity in so vitriolic and acerbic terms than Mongo Beti. In his novel *The poor Christ of Bomba*, Christianity is presented in a bad light, as a missionary endeavour that ends in disgrace and failure. He presents Christianity in doubt and uncertainty. The "Father" doubts the sincerity of all his roadside converts and the Christians wonder about Christianity. Mutual suspicion is rife. "I'm beginning to wonder myself whether the Christian religion really suits us, whether it's really made to the measure of the blacks. I used to believe it firmly, for didn't Jesus Christ say to his disciples, "Go and announce the Good tidings to all the peoples of the earth." But now I'm not so sure"[5] 'In Bomba where the girls were being prepared for Christian marriages, it became very clear why the girls had to stay in the women's camp for such long periods for the good of their souls or for the good of the mission building programme. Only gradually did it become clear that the local Churchmen were using the local girls for their own purposes[6]. Like the missionary outreach depicted in *The Whiteman of God*, the mission at Bomba ends on a sad note. There wasn't a sound any where, not a whiff of smoke; only a great silence as though the cemetery had gradually invaded the whole mission. Bomba had the look of an old abandoned village.[7]

The apparent failure of Catholicism in particular and Christianity in general and the reversion to traditional unchristian practice was one of the subjects of the pastoral letter on superstition by his Grace Archbishop Paul Verdzekov. The letter highlighted among other issues, a mentality prevalent among Christians which borders on syncretism. This dualistic and syncretic thought patterns prevalent among Christians is not moribund. It must be seen and acknowledged as an urgent issue and every Christian must give it the attention it deserves. He went on to say among other things that: it is perhaps to say that the first Christians of this diocese really and truly turned their backs on divination, charms and other superstitions...Today this seems to have changed completely. Divination, the use of charms and other superstitious practices are now rampant among many Christians. Many Christians are now leading what we must call a double life. They go to Church receive the sacraments and afterwards go the diviner to seek solutions, concerning illness, deaths, marriage problems, thefts or business problems, employment, promotion in their work place and so forth.[8] Sometimes in times of crisis the African Christian may offer a Mass intention and at the same time solicit the service of a soothsayer or marabous without any qualms of conscience. The experience in southern Nigeria was not different from what is obtained elsewhere. Many of those who came devoutly to Mass and the sacraments were living double lives, some were polygamists, and some were prostitutes, some practioners of pagan rites. Every one knew about it excerpt the missionaries.[9]

According to statistics the Population in Njinikom in 1927 was estimated at 1307 inhabitants but the size of Catholic community in Njinikom in the same year were 1741 inhabitants. This number of converts included converts out of Njinikom. This further blurs the fact and makes it difficult to know exactly what percentage of the population of Njinikom were Christians. There was never a time in Njinikom that traditional practices which were at odds with Christianity were completely eradicated. From its inception following the initial fervour some Christians failed to destroy what was regarded as pagan and unchristian. They gave Catholicism a trial hoping it would work. For example, the owner of the famous Juju masquerade known as Tokein became Christian but instead of destroying the objects he carefully kept them in the barn of his own house. Around the decade of the 1970's some people decided to bring to the open and to life this masquerade. The juju which was in hibernation was now in the open performing as it had once done before.

In another case it was a woman who had bags and pots of the native baptism known as the iking-i-wayn became a Christian and had the objects carefully stored away in the barn. Later on when there was some unusual form of sickness in the family the extended family approached her and everything came back to life as usual. Many Christians at the onset did not give up the pagan rites and rituals completely but simply gave Catholicism a trial when crisis were around the corner like the true African in times of crisis they naturally reverted to their old practices. Some might not have fully given up the practices of divination, sorcery and superstitions and when crisis cropped up they naturally went back to their roots.

In some cases at the death of one Christians the items were handed over to the one who was to inherit and what seems to have been at the point of extinction was been rejuvenated. Other Christians went back to the old cherished practice of polygamy; little by little other practices which seem to have hibernated for a time saw the light of day.

What went wrong in this adventure of flirting with Christianity? What loopholes might have prompted this attitude of reversion to practices that were incompatible with Christianity? Some Christians reverted to African Traditional Religion because they failed to realise some concrete help from the Christian faith. They might have embraced a juicy version of Christianity. Christianity for them was not pragmatic as it had presented from the onset. After the sudden death of a son or a Father or a relative some naturally reverted to look for solutions where they thought it was possible. Christianity had failed them woefully

Secondly the negative examples and influence of some Christians had negative effects on the zeal to practice Christianity. For example, the seizure of land or property by a nephew from the widow of the departed uncle was bound to cast doubts on the pragmatic nature of Christianity. Sometimes this was followed by the forceful eviction of a widow by one who was a Christian. Litigations in courts, which sometimes ended in a way that was considered unjust among other things gradually convinced many that Christianity was not worth its salt. This was compounded by scandalous lives of Christians. As a consequence some Christians and non Christians began to cast doubts on the efficacy of Christianity. Above all the inability of Christianity to shed light on genuine problems of the society which hitherto had been provided by soothsayers were enough reasons for the African to revert to African Traditional Religion.

What the early missionaries failed to do was to see African Traditional Religion as a religion at the dawn of the era of evangelization of this country. All over Africa certain terminologies coined by western anthropologists, especially following the dawn of the epoch marking publications of the works of Charles Darwin, Evans Pritchard, E.B. Taylor and Herbert Spencer which prevented many missionaries from perceiving and acknowledging the reality on the ground. The underpinning of the mentality of the colour bar gradually evolved into the coinage of derogatory and pejorative terms such as natives, savages, fetishes which were often employed to refer to Africans and their religion.

CALLS AND IMPORTANCE OF INCULTURATION

Unfortunately many prelates have taken this as a punch line against the missionaries but while doing practically very little themselves. Missionaries cannot be judged outside the confines of the spheres of thoughts of their time. In an article on Inculturation titled 'policy concerning the Use of Cameroonian Languages in the Liturgy and in Catechetic', Archbishop Paul went on to acknowledge this sad fact on the part of African prelates. "It is true that our Seminary formation did not prepare us for this. But with continued formation, we can liberate ourselves from the straitjacket of western formation, and squarely assume our responsibilities. I should like to underline very strongly the immense responsibility of Cameroonian priests to provide leadership in this question of the incarnation of the Christian Message. We are answerable to the Church and to history, Let us carefully go through the Documents referred to above, and ask ourselves whether we are not failing our people, our Missionaries and the Church by our apparent complacency in this all important matter of INCARNATION.[10]

Formerly it was fashionable for Africans to blame Missionaries and Rome for imposing a Western expression of Christianity on Africans, for inhibiting the emergence and evolution of African expressions of Christian Living and Worship, of denying to Africans the right to use their own languages, symbols, etc. in Christian Worship, and Catechetics. Today, no one will believe us anymore if we repeat such excuses. Rome has given us the widest possible opportunities for indigenisation. If we neglect to use these opportunities, the responsibility will lie squarely on our own shoulders. In fact, Rome is now irritated when Africans continue repeating the same old complaints of alleged Roman legalism inhibiting African creativity. Rome seems to be asking us: Who stops you from trying to express the one Faith according to the idiom, the genius, the language, the values, and the cultural heritage of your own peoples?[11]

This invitation and encouragement was not new, neither did it come from African prelates only. In line with the spirit of the Vatican II Council it became incumbent on missionaries to pursue the path of exposing the gospel in all its nakedness, stripping it bare of all its western wrappings. To neglect to pursue a policy of Incarnation would mean accepting and perpetuating that dramatic divorce between the Gospel and culture which the Holy Father so vehemently deplores in Evangelii Nuntiandi. It would mean accepting the unresolved conflict situation which thousands of Christians are living in their personalities due to the fact that the cultural substratum of their lives was never converted. This forces them to lead two lives concurrently. They are doomed to duality, and in crisis situations, they revert almost invariably and spontaneously to the "solutions" provided by their cultures, whether or not these are in conformity with the Gospel. We see this happening everyday among our practising Christians, including the very highly educated ones. It is the task of the clergy and of the Cameroonian priest in particular, to help overcome this situation which makes hybrids of our Christians by assisting our people to live their Christian lives in an integrated manner... Christianity cannot afford to stand outside a culture as something totally foreign or even alien to it. If the Cameroonian priest neglects his task of working out an indispensable synthesis, I am afraid that he will be judged severely by history; for such neglect will inevitably bring about syncretism, which we can already discern in our communities[12].

At Baptism, the African Christian repudiates remarkably little of his former non—Christian outlook. He may be obliged to turn his back upon certain traditional practices which the Church, rightly or wrongly has condemned in his area, but he is not asked to recant a religious philosophy. The Church, in any case, takes no cognizance of this philosophy. Consequently, he returns to the forbidden practices as occasion arises, with remarkable ease. Conversion to Christianity is for him sheer gain, an 'extra' for which he has opted. It is an overlay on his original religious culture. Apart from the superficial condemnations, Christianity has really had little to say about African Traditional Religion in the way of serious judgements of value. Consequently, the African Christian operates with two thought systems at once, and both of them are close to each other. Each is only superficially modified by the other. It becomes clear therefore; that the heart of the dialogue between Christianity and African Traditional Religion is located within the consciousness of the African Christian himself. It is there that the most serious exchange must take place.[13]

We are men marked by historicity, involved in culture. And as the Latin saying goes—Quid quid recipitur ad modum recipientis recipitur—whatever is received is received according to the mode of existence of the receiver. The Christian message must come to us as to people already immersed in a culture. This means that our immemorial customs, our pagan religion, our arts- dance, music, poetry, painting, sculpture must become baptised or somehow incorporated into our own type of Christianity, or else the history of our Church continues to be a mere gloss on European Church history, unless we are contented with no more than a skin-deep Christianity which our people abandon at the critical moments of their lives. We must come to terms with the implications of our involvement in culture. In the evangelisation of our people, we cannot continue to neglect our own culture to the detriment of our people"[14] and Christianity itself.

By reason of its deep conviction that "the synthesis between culture and faith is not only a demand of culture but also of faith", because "a faith that does not become culture is not fully accepted, not entirely thought out, not faithfully lived", the Special Assembly for Africa of the Synod of Bishops considered inculturation a priority and an urgent task in the life of Africa's particular Churches. Only in this way can the Gospel be firmly implanted in the Continent's Christian communities. Following in the footsteps of the Second Vatican Council, the Synod Fathers interpreted inculturation as a process that includes the whole of Christian existence—theology, liturgy, customs, structures—without of course compromising what is of divine right and the great discipline of the Church, confirmed in the course of centuries by remarkable fruits of virtue and heroism.[15] The challenge of inculturation in Africa consists in ensuring that the followers of Christ will ever more fully assimilate the Gospel message, while remaining faithful to all authentic African values. Inculturation of the faith in every area of Christian and human life is an arduous task which can only be carried out with the help of the Spirit of the Lord who leads the Church to the whole truth (cf. Jn 16:13).[16]

The Synod of African Bishops together with the Fathers of the synod rightly affirmed that "a serious concern for a true and balanced inculturation is necessary in order to avoid cultural confusion and alienation in our fast evolving society." During my visit to Malawi, I made the same point: "I put before you today a challenge—a challenge to reject a way of living which does not correspond to the best of your traditions, and your Christian faith. Many people in Africa look beyond Africa for the so-called 'freedom of the modern way of life.' Today I urge you to look inside yourselves. Look to the riches of your own traditions, look to the faith which we are celebrating in this assembly. Here you will find genuine freedom—here you will find Christ who will lead you to the truth."[17]

The issue of inculturation is not new. From the apostolic to the patristic times, from the patristic to the medieval age from Palestine to Rome, from Rome to the Franks and the vandals, from Portugal to South America and Far East Asia, the story has been the same. This dialogue between Christianity and culture can be seen in every age and every region.

THE CULTURAL DIALOGUE IN THE PATRISTIC ERA AND THE MIDDLE AGES

Like the complex pre paschal catechesis of Jesus (which was not simply the spoken word but also included action, attitude, gesture, silence, witness, suffering: "the total experience"), the post paschal catechesis about Jesus by the Apostles and the Christian community was highly articulated. It included preaching but also liturgical/sacramental and Eucharistic experience, expressed in everyday life. Communication of the faith was thus made complete through kerygma (the Word), leitourgia (the Sacraments, especially Baptism and the Eucharist), diakonia (service), koinonia-ekklesia (ecclesial communion), martyria (giving witness even through martyrdom).

In the patristic era, for example, there was a very lively cultural dialogue with stoicism and contemporary philosophical middle-Platonism. Non-Christian religions, which were rapidly multiplying in the Roman Empire at that time, also participated. Following the Greco-Roman example, even the grandiose conversions of the Germanic and Slavic peoples were modest attempts to inculturate the faith (with the adoption of practices, customs, language, legal behaviour, and religious expressions). Thus, the learned medieval summae can be considered not just innovative in methodology, but attempts to promote dialogue between Christianity, Islam, and Judaism. (cf., for example, the Summa contra Gentiles of St. Thomas Aquinas). The great schisms themselves, in the East (1054) and in the West (in the sixteenth century) can be viewed as the affirmations of different "cultural" conceptions and traditions of Christian experience by particular communities, eastern or western.

THE SIXTEENTH-CENTURY EVANGELIZATION OF THE AMERICAN INDIAN

More than anything else, missionary activity has been a proven source of evangelical inculturation. The evangelization of the American Indian in the sixteenth century, for example, represents an exemplary parable of the process of inculturating the Gospel. The missionaries rejected the models of Germanic and Slavic evangelization and hoped to imitate the style of true Apostles: to refrain from using weapons, to respect the laws of the peoples, to defend the rights of the native inhabitants, to study and adapt to their psychology, to become familiar with their religious beliefs. However, the Spanish colonizers were violent and dishonest: a painful thorn of counter-witness. Nonetheless, the fact remains that evangelization triumphed over immense problems.

INCULTURATION IN THE FAR EAST

Another significant example of inculturation of the faith in this period was the work of missionaries in the Far East, such as the Jesuits Robert de Nobili in India, Francis Xavier and Alessandro Valignano in Japan, and Michele Ruggieri and Matteo Ricci in China. Matteo Ricci made himself into "a Chinese man among the Chinese." He became fluent in the language and gave himself the Chinese name Li Madou. He assumed the clothing of a Confucian man of letters; he wrote books in Chinese and lived in Peking from 1601 until his death in 1610. His interpretation of certain Confucian rites was impressive, albeit completely misunderstood (for example, in Benedict XIV's apostolic constitution Ex quo singulari in 1742). These rites were, in his view, not so much expressions of religion, as of filial respect and piety between those who govern and their subjects, between Father and Son or husband and wife, between elder and younger brother, among friends, between the living and the dead.[18]

CRITERIA OF INCULTURATION
CHRISTOLOGICAL CRITERION
This is the first criterion of inculturation. Preaching the Gospel of Jesus Christ as a radical cure for human "nature" (fallen because of sin) and human culture by means of grace is an inculturation: "The law indeed was given through Moses; grace and truth came through Jesus Christ" (Jn 1:17). The inculturation process is actually a genuine incarnation of Christ and of his Gospel within a particular culture: "And the Word became flesh and lived among us" (Jn 1:14). Following the example of Christ, who judged and condemned the negative values of his time, the Gospel, too, continually evaluates the limitations and errors of the culture in which it exists. The reception given to the Gospel, the recognition of a culture's riches, and, at the same time, the purification or refusal of negative values enables a culture to rise and grow in a Christian way. The incarnation of the Gospel in a culture signifies the "conversion" of that culture to the Gospel and also the profound purification of that culture.

ECCLESIOLOGICAL CRITERION
Like Jesus, the Church lives in one time and place, in a particular society, in a specific culture. And, again like Jesus, the Church proclaims conversion to the Gospel to particular cultures (Mk 1:15). As the "body of Christ" (LG 7) and "sacrament of intimate union with God" (LG 1)—but also as a "community" and an "institution"—the universal and particular Church is thus, in history, the setting, agent, and guarantor for a true culmination of the inculturation process.

It is in the concrete reality of the life of the Church that inculturation is purified, carried out, and realized. For this reason, the historical Church is the setting for experiencing inculturation; it is the agency of inculturation; it governs the criteria for assessing the validity and legitimacy of inculturation. The post paschal Christian community was the first to use inculturation as an ecclesial experience of both welcome to and purification of the "Hebraic religious culture." Both worship (where "the breaking of bread" replaced the ceremonies of temple and synagogue) and behaviour saw the effects of this purification; circumcision was no longer imposed on converted pagans for this very reason (Acts 15:28-29): "For in Christ Jesus neither circumcision nor uncircumcision counts for anything; the only thing that counts is faith working through love" (Gal 5:6). The fundamental principle, however, remained the acceptance of authentic cultural values. Paul, for example, states: "Finally, beloved, whatever is true, whatever is honourable, whatever is just, whatever is pure, whatever is pleasing, whatever is commendable, if there is any excellence and if there is anything worthy of praise, think about these things" (Phil 4:8).

Distinguishing between faith and culture, between values and counter- values, is not always easy. Finding solutions is often arduous. Nevertheless, when they are adopted, they are to express the faith of the Church. That is why inculturation can be defined as an ecclesial method of incarnating and vitally re-expressing the Gospel, using a culture's own values, and purifying or denying those cultural realities that are opposed to the Gospel. Inculturation is a marvellous and mysterious exchange of gifts: "In one direction, the Gospel reveals to each culture the supreme truth of the values that the culture embodies and allows the culture to unleash that truth; in the other, each culture expresses the Gospel in an original way and reveals new aspects of it."

ANTHROPOLOGICAL CRITERION

According to this third criterion of inculturation, true evangelization becomes a grace-filled process of salvation of the human being, respecting the integrity of his nature and his culture. Conversion to Christ does not imply rejection of social or religious cultural values. On the contrary, conversion animates and fulfils these values in its gift of grace. Because each person is the object and the bearer of the Gospel, both as an individual and as a member of human and ecclesial society, inculturation reveals itself through the promotion and illumination of humanity and through the complete liberation of humanity from the negative realms of sin, death, injustice, meaninglessness, violence, poverty.

In his apostolic exhortation Catechesi tradendae, John Paul II describes the concept of inculturation this way: "The term 'acculturation' or 'inculturation' may be a neologism, but expresses very well one of the components of the great mystery of the Incarnation. We can say of catechism, as of evangelization in general, that it carries the strength of the Gospel to the heart of culture and cultures. For this reason, catechism will attempt to know these cultures and their essential components; it will learn their most significant expressions; it will respect their values and riches. In this way, catechism will be able to impart to these cultures the knowledge of the hidden mystery and to help them energize their own living tradition of giving original expression to Christian life, celebration, and thought" (no. 53).[19]

Writing on the importance of inculturation without precisely saying so, J.S. Mbiti went on to emphasis that; Unless Christianity and Islam fully occupy the whole person as much as, if not more than traditional religions do, most converts to these faiths will continue to revert to their beliefs and practices for perhaps six days a week, and certainly in times of emergency and crisis. The whole environment and the whole time must be occupied by religious meaning, so that at any moment and in any place, a person feels secure enough to act in a meaningful and religious consciousness. Since traditional religions occupy the whole person and the whole of his life, conversion to new religions like Christianity and Islam must embrace his language, thought patterns, fears, social relationships, attitudes and philosophical dispositions, if that conversion is to make a lasting impact upon the individual and his community.[20]

AFRICAN ATTEMPTS AT INCULTURATION

After the publication of the Post Synodal Exhortation Ecclesia in Africa the word inculturation and attempts at inculturation were in vogue. Many attempts were made to include local rhythms, songs, and symbols in the liturgy. Besides these attempts in the cultural sphere attempts were also made in literature. In *Ecclesia In Africa is Us, An attempt at Liturgical Inculturation for the Ecclesiastical Province of Bamenda*, Mbi and the inculturation committee of Muyuka Parish, went on to state emphatically which way was best for the Church to follow. They began by acknowledging the real problems of

Christianity in Africa today and why Christians regularly make use of African solutions by returning to their roots which may be at variance with Christianity when problems arise. Among the genuine needs of the African Christians is the desire to preserve life as the highest good. This is so because African Religion is pragmatic and utilitarian.

As if professing another creed Mbi and the Commission went on to say; we believe that what is called "country fashion" among our peoples, and indeed among every people, developed out of a legitimate struggle for survival. In the course of history our peoples encountered lots of difficulties. By the ingenuity of their leaders and with supernatural guidance they developed ways of overcoming the particular difficulties, which they encountered. In respect of the divinity that guided them, they preserved sacred traditions. This is how their various sacred customs came into being.[21]

There are several things that Jesus taught, which we, better than any other people in the world would be able to understand and express. To determine the prospect for an inculturated Christianity for our peoples what we need to do now is to explore the felt religious needs of our peoples and try to see what answers the gospel provides for these needs. If we are able to establish that the gospel can answer all the felt needs of our peoples then there is a high prospect for an inculturated Christianity for our peoples. If Christianity cannot answer the religious needs of our peoples then our effort at inculturation will be useless. The commission went on to identify the important needs of the people. They began by asking: What are the felt needs of our people? They went on to outline at length what these needs were.

> 1. Peoples want to live a normal, healthy, and full life here on earth. A simple example to illustrate this would be the rites of initiation that are performed for children. They want their children to be normal and healthy, they want their children to grow up and have a full life on earth. Where they find that this is not going to be the case experience has taught them that there are certain religious rites or "country fashion" that they need to perform to obtain this in the family. The child will be sickly and may die, perhaps only to be reborn again and again!

2. Secondly, people know that there is evil and wickedness in the world and witches and that wizards are responsible for a lot of this evil. Experience has taught them that they can perform certain rituals or "country fashion" in order to protect themselves, their property, and their land against the evil effects of witchcraft.

3. Peoples know that if the Ancestors are angry there can be no peace in the family. Experience again has taught them that if they perform certain religious rites i.e. "country fashion" the Ancestors will be appeased. Failure to do this will bring untold suffering to successive generations within the family.

These are some of the most important points in the daily life of many people and Western Christianity has not been able to fully address them. The cries of our peoples have been ignored and their age-old solutions, which gave them solace, have only met with rejection. Very little attempts even to understand and to assess the legitimacy of these cries have so far been made. Everything religious we do, every ritual we perform is simply condemned as "pagan."

Religion is meant, in a certain way, to assist people to face life. When it fails to do this they are left on the balance and go jumping between Church and country fashion, as if trying to find out which one helps them better.

Jesus said, "I have come so that they may have life and have it to the full" (Jn 10:10) He said he was sent to bring the good news to the poor, to proclaim liberty to captives and to the blind new sight, to set the downtrodden free ..." (Lk 4:19) Religion is life enhancing, it is not death dealing. Our efforts at inculturation will have lasting value if all that is truly life giving in our cultures is taken up and evangelized. If this does not happen then whatever we do in the name of liturgical inculturation will remain plastic, it will be a mimicking of rites that have real meaning only in our traditional culture.[22]

POSSIBLE AREAS OF INCULTURATION

After almost close to a century today a systematic study of pattern and worldview of the kom person will reveal to any one that as a people, they have a faith believed, faith lived, and faith celebrated. Sometimes because they are Christian (for those who have become Christians), some harbour thought patterns that border on syncretism. This is specifically so because the tenets of traditional religion lived, believed, and celebrated go along simultaneous with the Christian faith believed (creed) lived (commandments) and celebrated (liturgy). Certain aspects, which are incompatible, are harboured together giving rise to a dualistic and syncretic way of behaviour. It must be noted that like all African Traditional Religion not all aspects of the kom culture need to be purified by Christianity for they are by their nature and end intrinsically good. Some of these aspects are traditional marriage, matrilineal system of succession among others. Where are the areas where behaviour, thought system, and practices are dualistic and syncretic in nature and practice?

a) Sickness and Healing
b) Burial/ funeral rites
c) Ancestral Cult
d) Fertility Rites
e) Days of Rest and Obligation
f) Traditional Concepts and practice of Justice

There are Christians who have testimonies to give on the work of the evil one than on the work of God. They are proned to give testimonies on how God has apparently been defeated in their lives. Christianity for them does not carry the power it presupposes. Therefore, it is ritualistic and sterile. This way of thinking and action is prevalent in all spheres of life.

TRADITIONAL AND CHRISTIAN FUNERAL RITES

In all African societies, elaborate celebrations marking the departure of one into the world of the ancestors is a common feature. Funeral rites and burial rites have remained a cause of disagreement between the Church's authorities and some Christians as if these groups were separate portions of the Church. Funeral rites in the Church over the centuries have varied and today even among the African Churches; the customs of burial presents no uniform pattern. This thorny issue of burial of Christians has evolved over time in Archdiocese of Bamenda. From the period of the early missionaries, an evolution in the practice can be observed almost vacilitating between two poles.

The burial of Christians in a common place in the Church is an old practice dating back to the apostolic and patristic time. The word cemetery originally was Christian. It meant a sleeping place. A sleeping place for Christians, for those who had died in the Lord and who one day will be raised as the Church celebrates and proclaims in its liturgy. Common burial grounds at the same time can be cultural and have nothing to do with Christianity. In the early days of Christianity in the archdiocese of Bamenda, Christians were de facto buried in the Parish cemeteries. Christians were separated from the rest in many ways in life as well as at the end of their earthly life. This was one of the reasons why cemeteries were one of the visible signs of Christianity in a locality. At present, the story is not the same. In some Parishes, many of these cemeteries have long been abandoned.

From very early times, Christian communities set apart special grounds for the burial of Christians. These were Christian cemeteries. Christians, no matter from what family or tribe they came, knew that they were brothers and sisters. Deeply conscious of this unity, the early Christians decided that all departed Christians as members of one another, should be buried together in a Christian cemetery. The cemetery was very often quite close to the Church. In this way, Christians were reminded every day of their communion with the saints in heaven and the souls in purgatory.

Unfortunately, Christian cemeteries have been neglected very much in several parishes of this diocese over the last eighty years or more. Due to lack of care, some of our Christian cemeteries reverted into bush. And because of neglect on our part, many Christians started burying their Christian relatives in private compounds. The burial of Christians in private compounds has brought about many abuses.

Chapter Four: Present Day Challenges

The early Fathers and Christians of this Diocese did their best to observe these laws. They observed the Commemoration of all Souls by coming together for Holy Mass at the Parish Cemetery and by participating in some parts of the office of the Dead. Children, too, learnt to care for the graves of their departed relatives. Every Sunday, after Holy Mass, the entire Congregation went in procession to the Cemetery and prayed for the dead before going home. In this way, the teaching of the Church concerning the Communion of Saints was kept as a concrete reality in the daily lives of the Christians. When passing near a Cemetery, Christians remembered that they were passing near a holy place, and they remembered to say a short mental prayer for the faithful departed. Unfortunately, Christian cemeteries have been neglected very much in several Parishes of this Diocese. First, pagan rites influences and practices have now appeared at Christian burials. When Christians are buried outside of consecrated grounds, we should not be surprised if pagan influences tend to take over the burial. This Diocese is still, after all, overwhelmingly pagan. The Church does allow us to use, at burials, any good traditions that we may have, but anything alien to the Gospel must be changed. Secondly, burial in private compounds leads to the disappearance of the Christian Cemetery where all the members of God's Family in a given place are buried.[23] Twenty years before the emphasis on Christian cemeteries had been relegated to the background.

This tussle between Christian Cemeteries and traditional burial in compounds is not new. From the early years, the fight between the Church and traditional authorities has been a common feature. As far back as 1926 this controversy over burial places had started. For example, the queen mother Naya'a had fled kom because some of her brothers had been killed in a family dispute. Before her death as a Christian, she had given precise instructions on how and where she should be buried. After her death, the Fon protested to the civil authorities of the time. The Fon went on to remind Father Moran that he would accept the Church only if they allowed him to remove and re-bury the corpse of his mother. Father Moran worked out a compromise with the Divisional officer by which the Christians would bring the corpse in a procession and give it a Christian burial at the royal site. The peace making efforts of Father Moran were approved by the administration and paved the way for the re-opening of Njinikom in 1927.[24]

Kom traditional burial rites are influenced by certain beliefs. The people express their belief in their burial rites, which is indicative of its eschatological perspective. The belief in the form of life after death lies at the root of burial customs and rites. This final rite of passage has at its basis the belief in the form of life after death. African Traditional Religion is highly utilitarian in nature. Rites and ritual are performed to safeguard and to preserve life from all destructive forces. One of these destructive forces is the very parent who was alive and has now joined the world of the dead. While Christianity does not disregard the benefits of life on earth it is highly geared towards the life hereafter. One of the motives for Christians who backslide in this specific area is fear. Fear seems to be the main motive behind the efforts made often grudgingly by Christians to be at peace with their ancestors. The motive is far from being altruistic. When a person participates in the African Traditional Religious rite of burial and later funeral rites it is not out of love for the departed. It is often to forestall any mishap, which may befall one for failing to honour his obligation to the departed relative.

TRADITIONAL FUNNERAL RITES

Kom people have elaborate funeral rites that are performed during the burial of departed relatives. These rites and rituals differ from person to person and from lineage to lineage. These specific rites performed depend on how one has died and who has died. When a person is pronounced dead, burial arrangement may begin by laying the person in state. The traditional way of announcing the death of a person is by firing gunshots. Traditionally shrouds have been used since time immemorial. In the past calico was used. Calico was a coarse piece of cloth made out of the bark of a tree. From modern times with the coming of modern fabric, culture adjusted to accommodate what was modern. Even the number of shrouds was determined. Generally, the number of shrouds range from three to five shrouds. The five pieces of shrouds come from the following persons: the father of the deceased, the uncle, the son (if the deceased had one) the in-laws and the last one from the bed of the deceased. If the deceased had no children, three shrouds will be used: the father and the uncle will each supply one and the third will come from the bed of the deceased person. Furthermore, burial or funeral rites depend on the individual who has passed into the world beyond. In Kom, special rites are performed on bodies of members of secret societies, such as the Kwifon, traditional titleholders. These rites are performed by members of the cult to which he belonged.

A deceased usually is buried in one of his clothes and the other usually his finest, is given to his eldest son (child) or, in some instances, to the child who takes after him. Whoever wears the robes will be expected to remain in the outfit until the death celebration is over. The person is expected to imitate the deceased through out the celebration. Women related to the deceased are expected to prepare corn fufu which is the staple food in Kom, goats, chickens and gun powder are provided for by the men.

During the burial process in Kom, no specific words are used. In some cases, words may be used and rituals performed on the corpse. For example, when one dies mysteriously, when a young person dies and there are allegations that he/s has been killed. The person who is considered the suspect may be obliged to prove his innocence by undergoing trial by ordeal.

The grave is arranged in such a way that the casket is protected from soil. This is the reason why dry grass is put in the grave, be it the grave of a notable, a child or a woman. Some drinks (preferably alcoholic drinks) are given to those who dig the grave. Certain rites are performed before or after burial depending on the rank, the person had in the society. Formerly and in some cases today fresh grass is burnt to drive away the spirit of the deceased. Grass is consumed by people to protect them from more deaths, followed by the washing of hands as a sanitary measure.

An important rite, as far as funerals are concerned, is the offering of fowls by close relatives to the deceased person. This is done on top of the grave by plucking its feathers, accompanied by the invocation of the name of the deceased person. When a fowl is been sacrificed, the person offering the sacrifice calls on the departed by name and indicates that the fowl is meant for the departed relative in question. He may call as many departed relatives as possible with one fowl. There is nothing so specific to the kom people in these rites. For example, among the Ndebele, the animal killed afterward serves as it is said, to accompany the deceased, to provide him with food on the way and livestock in the next world. Drinking medicine usually made from ashes of burnt bones is a rite whereby the departed is mystically united with the members of his family and community who are still alive.[25]

When the initial rites are over, pieces of shrouds are distributed to the children and close relatives of the deceased. Family members who are expected to carry them on their arms. Some may make caps while others tie them round their necks. This is a traditional way of mourning a loved one. It was believed that if a person failed to have his or her hair shaved, he/s will be affected by Malaise during the day, but such a practice is dying out. Today, people no longer shave their hair as before. Others do it symbolically by trimming the edges of their hair or cutting off a few hairs. A white shroud may be used in the place of a blanket; the colour of the cloth may not be of much religious significance. The colour white is not mandatory and other colours may be used. A white piece of cloth may be used owing to the fact that it is less expensive than the blanket. On the other hand, white is used to show that the death person is clean and should not be soiled.

The sacrifices accompanying the deceased are performed meticulously. Such obligations are considered sacrosanct and one in his right frame of may not default. It is believed that if a family member dies and a surviving relative fails to carry out the expected funeral rites such as plucking of the feathers of fowls and slaughtering of goats, the person (deceased) may be troubled by other ancestors in the world beyond. The deceased will express his or her wrath by harming a particular individual who has failed to perform the sacrifice. The offended ancestor can only indicate his wrath or carry out his/her malevolent act on a family member of the deceased on the maternal side. The ancestors of one family cannot harm a person from another family. The deceased (it is believed) may not necessary indicate his displeasure with a malevolent act but with a simpler reminder. For example, "My uncle died in 1998 and we did not sacrifice the goats until 2005. Within the seven years we kept on seeing his ghost repeatedly until when we finally did the cry die. I do not know whether it is some one in this world who use to take up the face of our uncle in his witchcraft act and came to us as our late uncle or it was actually our uncle. My father died in 2006 all the rites performed. Today in the year 2010 we have not experienced any mishap nor have we seen his ghost. On the contrary my step brothers who did not give the requirements are seeing the ghost of our father, they fall sick time and again"[26].

It was and is still customary to apply cam wood on the corpse. The application of cam wood on corpses was at first, a symbol of honour. This practice was not general among the clans that made up the kom tribe but it was initially limited to two clans of the kom people. These families applied cam wood on their corpses. As the practice continued down the ages, it began to spread to all the families in Kom. This was a sign of honour. It should be noted that this practice of adorning with cam wood is not limited to corpses. During funerals, the grand daughters are adorned with cam wood as well. It is used to honour a person either dead or alive. It is used to adorn a mother after birth, the bride, and her attendants during traditional wedding ceremonies and in the performance of some sacrifices in the tribe. In the past, the practice whereby the hands of the deceased person were washed with water flowing through and down to those of his descendants was common. It was believed that after rubbing the corpse with cam wood, hands had to be washed and by doing so blessings flowed from the deceased to his/her descendants.

Traditionally more honour is accorded to elderly and titled men but this is not the case with commoners. Secondly, members of juju societies are buried in a specific way. Gravediggers assemble in the morning of the burial day with drums and xylophones. Male relatives of the deceased are expected to take part in digging the grave. Graves are dug in the same spirit that governs estimates of age. Sticks are used to cover the shelf at the bottom of the sixth, seventh, eight or ninth foot in the grave, where the corpse usually rests, tucked safely under the veranda of the house in order to protect it from rain. Quarter jujus[27] are present to animate the occasion. Jujus usually preside at the burial especially those in which the deceased belonged. Sometime, the jujus prepare the corpse for burial; warn witches to stop their mischief and equally help in settling disputes. Usually, jujus give the command for the corpse to be moved to the burial site. When the corpse is removed from the house usually by jujus, others stand outside brandishing their spears and cutlasses. Men inspect their guns to see if everything is in order and when the lower end of the coffin appears at the doorway, guns are fired. Kom people hold that shooting a gun is a man's way of crying and that women may cry. Jujus usually carry the coffin with the corpse in a slow counter clockwise procession around the central area of the compound to show their respect for the deceased. Ordinary people who die are carried by their children and not jujus and the corpse is usually taken directly from the house to the grave.

The famous juju on its way to a death celebration. In the background is the Catholic Church in Fundong. The point of divergence regarding jujus between the Church and tradition have remained one of the most difficult and insurmountable obstacles to a complete conversion to Christianity.

As the corpse is lowered into the grave, women wave at the coffin of the deceased as a sign of their last greetings. Women make thrilling noises, as a substitute for crying. This is reserved for old people who die. Drummers and xylophonist usually intensify and vary the beats to synchronise with the mood of the moment as gunshots are fired. These gravediggers are given beer to drink after the task has been completed. When this is done, the juju to which the deceased belonged during his earthly life will ask the eldest son to gather everybody by the gravesite (relatives of the deceased). Each will say goodbye and others will ask the deceased to greet those who in the lineage who have joined the world of the ancestors. This usually ends the burial ceremony.

However, the burial is only a preliminary to the celebration commonly known as the "cry die." The death celebration is often on the third day, the day for jujus to display. Jujus from the palace are the most important jujus in Kom land. The second day is usually spent preparing for the third day. All those concerned usually assembled on the eve of the third day with the Chong, the men's society that presides over death celebrations. At death celebrations, the members of the Chong society sit up all night playing their friction drums and receiving goats and chickens. Whenever, 'Chong' arrives at a death celebration; they are usually greeted with a fowl. The person "crying the die" brings an animal and announces the name of the deceased. Each of the deceased's sons and the maternal nephews presents the goats to the Chong society. Some of the goats are called 'real goats', 'substituted goats' and 'goats in kind' (goats in kind are money that represents the price of a goat).

At midnight, the head of the family must come and say good night to the Chong members, (when this was still done in the night) by bringing three fowls. In the morning, he brings another fowl to say good morning. When the celebration ends, he gives one more fowl to say goodbye. The end of the celebration is usually signalled by the Chong society. Xylophones and other instrument of juju society are played throughout the eve of the celebration. In the case of a 'Chindo', the first juju that usually displays on the 3rd day is usually from the palace. If a juju is entitled to seven fowls, it cannot be given six or eight. Jujus that have long histories usually require specific entertainment. Some of the jujus are ranked according to the status of their owner. The most ranked jujus in Kom are those from the palace.

However, the jujus represent the social world of the Kom people. Some jujus are destructive, others demanding and others are good. All Jujus portray different aspects of the Kom culture. Haircut is usually on the fourth day. Very early in the morning of the fourth day cooked groundnut mixed with corn is shared to all family members available. It is believed in kom land that the first person who deeps his hand in to the basket where the mixed corn and groundnut is put is the deceased one and after having his share of the food he takes off for the land of the ancestors. Enthroning of the successor on the fourth day and sometimes later. Close family member returning to their various homes after the affairs of the fourth day.

When one's maternal family is celebrating a funeral, all those eligible to give goats are expected to honour their obligation. An inventory of those who have brought their goats and those who have not is usually done. Those who have not brought their goats may not be required to do so immediately. They are expected to honour this obligation during the next family funeral celebration. Here note is taken by the family elders. When a person's father dies, the village takes the inventory of goats. If a deceased person had five sons and only three give their goats during his death celebration note is taken by the village that the other two sons owe the village. Those giving them must spell out to the family the names of the dead on whose behalf the goats have been given. After the goats are received both from the maternal family and sons of a deceased in the Ndo-Chong the goats are taken out for slaughtering without any other act performed on the goats again. Those giving them mention the names of the deceased over the chickens and the goats. When one loses a friend or a family member on the maternal or paternal line he simply get a chicken and takes it to the person's maternal family and simply say that this is so-so and so person's chicken that has been brought and it ends there. The goats pay back to the village what your deceased one ate in the village during his life time, while the role of the chicken is to feed the numerous people who have come to bury or (cry the die) of your late one

Honour paid to the death is also along gender lines. Traditionally women have their way of paying their dues to their departed mothers. In the kom culture, it is through what is known as "ingkuo."(Literally meaning basket). Men offer sacrifices to the departed relatives be they male or female. Women however are expected to pay their respect to their mothers, which may be done later. Funeral rites are complex. What has been written in the above paragraphs depict to a large extent the main highlights and elements which fall under the ordinary death celebration.

TRADITIONAL FEMINE RITES

The aim of most religious rites is to placate and court the supernatural to solve problems arising from events, which may not be easily understood. Like all sacrifices, this one is pragmatic and utilitarian. Its origin lies in the period of social disturbances. Historically there were period of intertribal wars, famine, slavery and epidemics which led to the death of many kom people. These led to social unrest, causing the dispersion of families. When peace and security returned, survivors decided to come together. Mass deaths are likely to be occasions of religious revival as well as time to examine the fate of those who have gone ahead. The concept of feeding and appeasing the departed relatives lies at the root of the origin of this rite. Consequently, the surviving relatives did this feeding of the departed relative communally by contribution of food items. After the contribution, they were all expected to gather to feast, believing that their late ones were also doing likewise in the world beyond. This practice continued down the line with minor additions and omissions down to the present day.

The eldest daughter of the departed woman usually performs this "ingkuo" rite. However, the other daughters are also obliged to perform the rite in their respective villages after marriage. The main reason why the other daughters perform the rite is in order that they may be given a chance to take part in similar ceremonies in their own villages. It is not obligatory for the other daughters to perform such a rite in honour of their departed mother but it is an obligation for the eldest daughters. Those who can take part in this rite are those who have once performed the rite. Funeral rites in general have no form of initiation. It is certain that the eldest daughter has to perform the rite after her mother's death. If the eldest daughter dies without performing the rite, the second eldest automatically takes over the responsibilities and the chain continues as such. Where the departed woman had no female children, nieces to the deceased woman may perform the rite.

Like all rituals in African Traditional Religion, this rite is performed solely to sustain development and save lives. It is believed that if the dead were not fed, they would cause poor growth of food crops, which may lead to a very low yield for the family in question. After performing this rite, the family is expected to be blessed with a very great harvest and no misfortune is expected to befall any of the family members. On the contrary, failure to perform the rite will lead to a myriad of problems: poverty, hunger, destruction of food crop by wild animals, lightning striking some of the family members, a worker going bankrupt, frequent sickness without cause, a string of deaths in the family or an ancestor manifesting his wrath by causing the grave to subside or cracks to appear on the grave among others.

With respect to the actual celebration of the rite, the initial preparation begins with the invitation of the elders on the eve of the occasion. Corn beer is prepared, alongside small quantities of corn fufu for the "elders" to eat. The woman who is to perform the rite is expected to assemble the following items: 20 litres of oil, a bag of salt, corn flour, bitter leaves, and two to three kilograms of meat and approximately 5 - 7 buckets of corn (amended to four in modern day by the Kwifon). The sisters and female cousins of the woman in question supplement this. In the case of a younger daughter performing the rite, her husband is expected to contribute. Later, these items are assembled, the corn beer preserved in special calabashes in preparation for the next day.

On the day proper, the elders come as early as possible, each coming along with small basket of corn. The corn is poured into a large basket, which can hold up to 10 buckets of corn. This basket is placed at the centre of the floor. Meanwhile in the course of this preparation the elders may entertain themselves with corn beer, fufu corn with bitter herbs. The meat is cooked with the bitter herbs. The central rite of this ritual is the most important. When corn flour is about to be put into the boiling water, the woman concerned will call on the ancestors, starting with the name of the person the rite is meant principally for and then followed by the naming of other late family members from the oldest to the youngest. After this naming, all the corn flour is poured in to the boiling water, which is used to prepare the corn fufu. When the food is ready, the corn fufu, bitter leaf, oil, and salt are shared among the participants. In case where any of the items is absent, for example, oil, everything will be done as expected but the oil distribution session is postponed. By so doing, the woman is exempted from collecting what she did not afford on her own day to distribute to the "elders" if she were to take part in a similar occasion elsewhere. If the woman in question is unable to afford what is required, she loses the right of receiving such items in any occasion of "ingkuo" rite in the village.

When all the items have been distributed, there comes a stage called "ndabah" when all family members beginning from the eldest to the youngest, male and female are invited to come in and make some small contributions of money in the form of an offering. This money is distributed among the elders. The reason put forward for the "ndabah" is simple: the late mother, who smoked a pipe when she was alive, will definitely need some tobacco to fill her pipe in the world of the dead; hence the name "ndabah" which literally means tobacco.

AFRICAN AND CHRISTIAN RELIGIOUS UNDERPINNINGS OF FUNNERAL RITES AND POINTS OF DIVERGENCE AND CONVERGENCE

Burials and funerals are key moments to test the faith of Christians specifically in the belief in life after death. It is also one of the areas where African Traditional Religion and Christianity conflict. A funeral Mass is celebrated with all the blessings, which portray vividly the expression of Christian faith in the heavenly inheritance as well as resurrection. In Church, the Christians commend the departed to the mercy of God and accompanying Masses are offered. At home, all the traditional rites are performed to forestall any eventualities that may arise from failure to perform these burial and funeral rites. Even the place of burial is sometimes a cause of disagreement. Many of the problems do not begin when a person dies. A good number of Christians who occupy prominent positions in Church may have been or are in prominent positions in societies whose creed is at variance with Christian faith and practice. In some cases, Christians continue to exercise such functions in church and maintain a similar if not active presence in these groups.

The Polemics do not end with the burial of a person as such. Many sacrifices in African Traditional Religion are connected with a departed relative. When misfortune strikes, if the source cannot be found among human beings, then the ancestors are the likely source. This is one of the reasons why people will go to any length to offer sacrifices and celebrate a string of death celebrations to make sure that the broken communion with an ancestor is restored. "In all African societies, there are myths about the presence of evil spirits of the deceased can have a strong influence on an individual's life by causing disaster to those who forget them in their daily life or leave them out of life's events. When there is a problem in the family, a failure in the son's exams, successive deaths of newborn babies among others, the family member can suspect that the spirit of a dead parent or grandparent is reproaching the family for failing to honour his obligation. In such situations, sacrificial offerings are made. The sacrifices serve to rebuild the relationship with the ancestors and to repair the damage caused to others. It is also a means of obtaining kindness and protection from spirits of the departed. The fear of death both biological and spiritual pushes the

African to unite intimately with the spirits who are on their way to eternity. The spirits understood this way live together with human beings in the same geographical area and fight with them against their enemies."[28]

Closely connected to burial and funeral rite is the belief in the last things. Eschatology plays an important part in both Christian and African Religion. However, there is a fundamental difference. "In African Traditional Religion the concept and belief in heaven and hell are foreign. There is neither a paradise to be hoped for nor hell to be feared in the hereafter. The soul of man does not long for spiritual redemption or closer contact with God in the next world"[29]. The ancestors remain present in the mind and daily life of Africans. What Christianity has failed to do is to reconcile certain beliefs accruing from experience of the African Christian with contemporary Christianity. Religion in general helps in making certain phenomenon comprehensible. When a religion fails to make certain phenomena arising from people's experiences understandable and fails to provide the means to overcome them, the possibility of complete and total adherence to it reduces or remains far-fetched.

This is the crux of the matter and lies at the root of double living by Christians. Certain questions concerning the spirit of the dead, their mode of existence, their ability to harm the living ranks among the common worries of Christians. This is partly the reason why the eradication of certain funeral rites, sacrifices to ward off angry ancestors has remained unsuccessful. Unless and until Christianity successfully penetrates this area of African Traditional Religion regarding ancestors, evil spirits, witchcraft, necromancy, sorcery and convincingly overcome and defeat any doubts, lip service to Christianity will continue to persist.

In Ecclesia in Africa is Us, An attempt at Liturgical Inculturation for the Ecclesiastical Province of Bamenda, Mbi and the inculturation committee of Muyuka Parish, suggests a way out for such a benign, irksome problem. They went on to say that the Eucharistic liturgy is a sacrifice, a much worthier sacrifice than the goats' blood and fowls' blood, which we offer traditionally (Heb 10:4). Peoples know from experience, however, that offering Mass for a dead relative does not take away the need to go back home and make "country fashion." Ancestors do not recognize the Eucharist. Even if one offers a thousand Masses, they would continue to trouble the surviving relative until the traditional fowl or goat is offered. Efforts at inculturation will truly succeed only if ancestors, whether they were Christians in this life or not, recognize the Eucharist as a valid sacrifice and accept it.

This is crucial because the Ancestors are the custodians of culture and religion. They have, as it were, the power to bind and loose. What they accept as valid will be valid and peoples will do it if necessary. Furthermore, what they reject will remain rejected and peoples will not do it. The question, therefore, is to find out if it is possible for the Ancestors to accept the Eucharist.

Priests who have the pastoral care of souls can testify that people do not cherish funeral Masses. More often than not, there is a struggle between the so-called "pagans" and the Christians. Those who insist on bringing their dead person to Church are devoted Christians, and they are in the minority. The rest may agree but it is more often for them a show than a necessity.

It is important to stress that traditional religion and culture have developed in the course of the centuries as a response to some specific needs. It has not remained the same. Important things have changed with the approval of the Ancestors. In many tribes, human sacrifices were common in the early days. In the course of time, animal sacrifices came to replace human sacrifices. What necessitated this change? At a certain point, peoples came to realize that it was immoral to sacrifice people. They turned to the Ancestors in prayer and got the permission to immolate animals instead. In most cases, the Ancestors themselves indicated what animals were to replace the human victim. Today we know of Christian Fons who have refrained from immolating animals and have used cam wood dye to signify the presence of blood.

The Eucharist is a sacrament, a sacred sign, and a non-bloody re-enactment of a bloody sacrifice. We are morally certain that if the Ancestors are informed of the value of the Christian Eucharistic sacrifice they will accept it. The dead do not really need goats, fowls or any material presents which the living offer to them. What they really get out of the sacrifice is the recognition of the assembly. The goats and fowls that we immolate are rather for the living. Abraham had to learn a similar lesson when in a bid to test his faith

God asked him to sacrifice his son Isaac (Gen.22). Among the Mbo/Bakossi, the story is that in past slaves used to be offered in sacrifice. After some time, there were no more slaves and so the people began to offer their own sons. However, they soon realized that the population was dwindling. An appeal was made to the Ancestors through a special ritual and the goat was shown to the people as the animal that was to replace the human victim.

It is important that recognition be given to the ancestors. They need it, and that is why they ask for it. In the Christian faith, we know that the saints and Angels in heaven are glorified to the extent to which we honour them on earth. It is, therefore, not incompatible with the Christian faith to give honour to our ancestors. The Holy Father has already mentioned that the veneration of our Ancestors is in some way a preparation for belief in the communion of Saints (Ecclesia in Africa no.43). We should bring them into the sacred liturgy. To do this we may have to rethink the place where we shall celebrate the Eucharist in honour of the Ancestors. We may have to rethink the hour of day or night when the immediate family can be fully involved as it is the custom. We may have to rethink the point of feeding the people and make room for it. When all this is done and culture would have been Christianized and our faith acculturated.

The worldview of the westerner, which we have seen, is very good and has many advantages, which are quite visible in technological progress. It is a worldview that is efficient. In this way, the west has a lot to offer to the world. Worship that is forged out of the western vision of reality is very good and expresses what is good in the Good News, which Jesus taught us. The worldview of the African, which we have seen is also very good and has many advantages for the spiritual life of our peoples. A worldview is more dynamic and existential. Worship that is forged out of the worldview of the African is very good and will surely bring out some elements of what Jesus taught us which western worship is unable to express.

Just as both these conceptions of reality have advantages and disadvantages. The effects of original sin are present everywhere. Western thought and worship lends itself to materialism and individualism, while African thought lends itself to superstition and fear. Which one is a lesser sin? The Good News shall always have something to counteract. What can we say? In this human condition, no culture is perfect and so no liturgy can ever be perfect. The good thing in having an African liturgy and in inculturating faith lies in those values which give meaning to our being, will be highlighted and developed. In this way, that which is best in us will be given expression. People feel awkward and out of place when personal needs are dismissed as superstitious and foolish. With inculturation, people appreciate Christianity better. This is the only way people will feel truly at home in the Church.

Difficult as it is, inculturation is not impossible. It opens up a new direction for the development of traditional religion and culture The Ancestors, who are the custodians of culture and traditional religion, must be given the recognition, which they deserve. When this is done, they will accept Christian practice into the culture. Let us carry on with our work and see what comes out.[30]

The suggestion that if the ancestors are informed of the value of the Christian Eucharistic sacrifice, their presence invoked, the people feed in their honour, they will accept for it is important that we give them the recognition if not they will ask for it may sound like syncretism. Many Christians often blame the apparent intransigence on the part of the Church on the formation of its clergy. Nothing is new under the sun. What African Christians are facing today is the same problem the early Christians had to battle with. St. Augustine in his Confessions on food and drink offered to the dead offers some advice on this matter. "My mother brought meat and bread and wine to the tombs of the saints as was her custom in Africa, but the door keeper prevented her to carry them in. When she found that the custom was prevented by so famous a preacher and so pious a Bishop even to those who used it soberly-both that no occasion of drunkenness should be given to those tending to excess and also because these funeral feasts were too much like the superstitions of the pagans in honour of their dead ancestors- she abandoned her practice most willingly. In her basket filled with the fruits of the earth, she learnt to offer at the tombs a heart full of better desires, namely that she was able to give what she could to the needy, and that the communion of the lord's Body was celebrated when the martyrs has been sacrificed and crowned in the imitation of his passion.[31]

It is customary that people do not visit one's compound and go with away with empty stomachs. Feeding the people is a commendable act and a sign of Christian charity. However, the feeding of the people is after the central rite has been performed. It is this central rite, which involves the offering of the fowls and goats with the naming of the ancestors that is at odds with Christian faith. Nothing is new under the sun, the practice of offering food and drink to the dead was a problem even at the time of St. Augustine. The practice of offering food or drink or pouring libation is widespread and not limited to any specific African tribe. Concerning the nature of honour which Christians pay their martyrs, St Augustine writes; "which Christian ever heard a priest standing before an altar built for the honour and worship of God over the holy body of a martyr, say in his prayers: "I offer this sacrifice to you Peter, or to you Paul, or to you Cyprian" No; at the tombs of these martyrs the sacrifice is offered to God alone, who made them first men and finally associated them with his holy angels in heavenly honour".[32]

An analysis of the movement of the sacrifice of the Mass and the ancestral cult reveals certain nuances between the two. The consecration rite during Eucharistic Celebration calls on the lord to bless and approve our offering so that it may become His body and blood but in ancestral sacrifice, a particular ancestor, or group of ancestors are called upon to receive a chicken or goat etc. In one, the lord accomplishes a mystery but in the other, a surviving relative gives some thing to a departed relative. The suggestion that ancestors should be called to accept the sacrifice of the Eucharist puts the ancestors out of the realm of the saints, it is balkanisation and at the same time africanisation, if not "tribalisation" ,of the eschatological realm. It puts the sacrifice of the Mass out of the reach of the departed relative who by their lives merited eternal salvation. It places the one who is to demand that ancestors accept the sacrifice of the Mass on a high moral ground capable of deciding the gymnastics of the spiritual realm. It places the surviving relatives at the mercy of the ancestors. Above all it makes the sacrifice of the Eucharist ineffective and foreign to the ancestors.

In many instances, many Africans at the dawn of the era of evangelisation refused baptism because of the balkanisation of the eschatological realm. Many believed that if they were baptised they would be spiritually and eternally made incapable of seeing their spouse. Baptism automatically removed them from the realm of Africans to the realm of Europeans in the spiritual sphere. Others grudgingly gave in to baptism afraid that baptism would make them not to be recognised in the next world by their relatives. This mentality does not end here; it has its underpinnings reflected in a symptomatic way in numerous sacrifices offered to the dead.

Another solution to this problem comes from the erstwhile and estranged Archbishop Emmanuel Milingo in *The world in between Christian Healing and Struggle for Spiritual Survival*. For him, the answer is Jesus and "I am certain that the Africans will do the sifting of their religious values when they come across the power of Jesus. It would not be strange for them to carry Jesus in the place of their living dead ancestors by whom they are used to being possessed... they will give way when Jesus comes in provided that Jesus guarantees protection and guardianship to the living members of the clans and tribes. He will undoubtedly do so with pleasure"[33].

The communion of saints occupies an important place in Catholic tradition. We believe in the communion of saints, whether these still make their pilgrim way on earth, whether, their life over, they undergo purification or they enjoy the happiness of heaven. All, they go to form the one Church. We likewise believe that in this communion, we are surrounded by a love of a compassionate God and his saints, who always listen to our prayers, even as Jesus told us, ask and you shall receive.[34] In full consciousness of the whole mystical body of Jesus Christ, the Church in its pilgrims members, from the very earliest days of the Christian religion, has honoured with great respect the memory of the dead; and "because it is a holy and wholesome thought to pray for the dead that they might be loosed from the sins" she offers suffrages for them[35]

A memorial service begins normally with the Eucharistic celebration with special intention for the specific departed person. If the person had been buried in the cemetery, as is the current practice, the priest proceeds to the cemetery with the congregation for blessings and lying of the wreath following by the lighting of the candle.

One can rightly say that the departed has been remembered and honoured. People have met and communion in his or her name. Like any sacrifice the significance lies in the central rite. This is precisely the fundamental difference between a Christian memorial service and a traditional death celebration. Though Christianity and traditional death celebration have some areas of communality in the area of eschatology, African Traditional Religion is grossly deficient. In the area of honour paid to the death, African Traditional Religion does not discriminate or sift ancestors along lines of righteousness or unrighteousness. Nonetheless, ancestors are sometimes, besides the way they died distinguished by the way, they manifest their wrath or displeasure in the event of a surviving relative falling in his obligation to the ancestors. It is generally believed that evil ancestors manifest their wrath violently leaving the surviving relative no room to make amends. Good ancestors like good parents will patiently send warning signals benevolently urging the surviving relative to come to his senses and honour his obligation. It can be said generally that ancestors are honoured and appeased without much recourse to the way the lived their lives or their abode or mode of existence. Christianity leaves no room for such ambiguity. In the eschatological realm, there is no neutrality. You are either with God or without God.

What happens before one knows with certainty that a departed relative is demanding a sacrifice, what are the departed really looking for? For the African the signs are many, sudden sickness, failure of his son in an exams, cracks appearing on the grave of the departed relative, a string of deaths or even one death. The polemics surrounding honour paid to the dead touches on fundamental aspects of Christian faith, which are non-negotiable- the salvific mission of Jesus, his lordship and its cosmic significance. It is customary in Cameroon to celebrate Mass in some places in the cemetery. The month of November in the universal church has been set aside to pray for the dead. One may ask if this remembrance is not enough or if families were to gather in family Masses to pray for their departed would that not suffice.

In African Traditional Religion, the concept of collective immortality is very crucial in the understanding the African eschatological realm. One lives as long as those who know him are alive. When the particular person who knew a living dead also dies, it is no longer necessary to pay close attention to him in family obligations of making offerings and libations. For a few years now, the notion of memorial service has begun to gain grounds. The relatives of the departed on the anniversary would offer a Mass and invite friends to celebrate the life of their departed relative. What recognition do the ancestors want? Some hold the view that ancestors need blood to live in the world beyond. A general study of other cultures in the area of sacrifices for the dead leaves us convinced that there must be some other reason. Any debate or research on the paranormal sphere is very delicate and difficult. What is the value of sacrifice on behalf of the dead? Do they need blood to survive in the world beyond? Not many people will agree with those who hold the view that the dead need blood to survive. I do not see with the person in this light because every person on earth has blood in his system. If blood was to help the dead live in the world beyond what happens to those persons in cultures where in place of chicken, goat, cow, pig, vegetable or kola nuts are offered. How will they live in the world beyond with vegetable water and kola nuts? I admit I do not know if the ghost of my relative was real or was the work of witchcraft because I live in one world and not the two at a time. Ghost, witchcraft, demon all is real. My father (before he died) was with me in my house; three hours before his death he said and I quote, (you people should give them sufficient food and healthy goats so that they should take home sufficient meat). Three hours before he died, he was already between the world beyond and ours here. If blood were necessary in the world beyond, he would have mentioned it.[36] We are dealing with the paranormal and humans are deficient in this area by nature.

Sometimes, Africans have the misconception that the African spiritual world is different and limited to the Africans; that the European has no problems with the spiritual world. The first book of Samuel describes the encounter between Saul and Samuel. Saul the king of Israel had gone to consult Samuel who was long dead with the help of a medium. Saul received nothing but a rebuke and a deadly promise of his impending death.[37] At the time, the Catholic Church in Nigeria began thinking that it was not right to have buried Bishop Shanahan out of the Church he had founded. Father Joe

Delaney said Shanahan had appeared to him on several occasions and he took it as a sign that he wanted to be buried in Nigeria. Nevertheless, Delaney was not taken seriously by the priests; among them, Archbishop Heerey. At last, he appeared to Heerey himself. In a letter to Sister Brigid Ryan, Archbishop Heerey described what happened.

..I was going up to my room after my last visit to the lord about 9:30pm. I switched on the light at the bottom of the stairs- and there he was, as clear as ever he appeared during his life, standing looking down on me, in white soutane, purple cincture, a pectoral cross and all, as he was well known to us. He had a serene sympathetic look as if to convey to me that he understood the whole situation. I had not been thinking of him at all.[38]

Sacrifice and offering to the departed is nothing peculiar to the kom people neither is the attempt by the Church to discourage it new. The Christians of the first centuries had the same dilemma to face. The number of Christians who frequently indulge in this practice is not negligible. The practice seems never to have gone away. What solutions have been put forward by the Church leaders? In the past when the Church leadership and reflection were largely European it was commonplace to condemn it in hard terns as paganism. Even nowadays, the word pagan has gradually been filtered out of the general vocabulary. Since the Church became indigenous in its personnel and leadership, the scholarly and current waves of reflection have hinted on how this seemingly benign and aching problem can be tackled once and for all. Current recognition of African Traditional Religion has led to the initiation of dialogue, dialogue not as equal partners but dialogue as a means of evangelisation.

The introduction of the concept of Christ as our ancestor has not been fully exploited. The living dead are still people; they are the guardians of family affairs, traditions, ethics, and activities. Offence in these matters is ultimately an offence against the ancestors who, in the capacity, act as invisible police of the family and communities. They know the needs of men, they have recently been here with men and God, and at the same time, they have access to the channel of communicating with God directly. Therefore, men approach them more often for minor needs of life than they approach

God. Even if the living dead do not do miracles or extraordinary things to remedy the need, men experience a sense of psychological relief when they pour out their heart's trouble before their seniors who have one foot in both worlds[39]. Christ as our ancestor fits, very well with "have recently been here with men and God and at the same time they have access to the channel of communicating with God directly"[40] The role of Christ encompasses and over shadows even the role of the ancestors.

It is sometimes common to hear a person who was present during the last moments of a departed relative saying that prior to the final departure of the deceased the deceased had said he saw one or two departed relatives coming to take him or her away. The person seems to be living in the two worlds at the same time able to communicate to those in both. This is nothing new nor is it an African phenomenon. Prior to his death Shanahan's Countenance was described in the following words: his face became transfigured, glowing with beauty and love and he seemed to listen to some unheard sound. When he came back to himself he said; did you not see them? Our Holy Mother and her divine son. They will come for me soon.[41]

In expressing the consciousness of faith, the second Vatican Council teaches that, "the word of God through whom all things were made, was made flesh, so that as perfect man he could save all men and sum up all things in himself. The lord is the goal of human history, the focal point of all desires of history and civilisation, the centre of humanity, the joy of all hearts and the fulfilment of all aspirations. It is him who the Father raised from the dead, exalted and placed at his right hand, constituting him judge of the living and the dead." It is absolutely this uniqueness of Christ, which gives him an absolute and universal significance whereby, while belonging to history, he remains history's centre and goal. I am the Alpha and the Omega, the first and the last, the beginning and the end."[42]

AFRICAN FORMS OF HEALING
INTRODUCTION

People want to live a normal, healthy, and full life here on earth. A simple example to illustrate this would be that they want their children to grow up and have a full life on earth. When they find that things are not going to be the case, experience has taught them that there are certain religious rites or "country fashion" they need to perform to obtain this in the family. The difference between western Christianity and the African vision is founded on western Platonic dualism. For the African vision, all of reality is one whole, whereas, western Christianity maintains a duality between body and soul, heaven and earth etc. With this duality, the soul is to be redeemed from the body and from life on earth. Attention is given to a life of happiness in a future heaven. For now, we have to endure suffering in this vale of tears. Such an approach to life and to religion does not have much appeal.[43] This struggle for survival has over the years gradually brought into existence rites and rituals whose sole aim is the restoration of health. The kom people have among these rites and rituals the Ikeng-I-wayn and the Ise. The former is family based while the later is communal in character.

IKING I WAYN

Iking I wayn is a sacrificial rite which is performed for children. The word "ikeng" refers to the pot in which these rites are performed. It is also called "fiyinifi wayn," i.e. the god of the child. It is alleged that the first people to introduce it in Kom land were those from the clan of "Igayn." These people were those who first settled in Kom land. Reports also say that it was the gods of a certain lake found at the boundary between Kom land and the land of Bafmeng, who requested that this rite be instituted. This Ikeng Iwayn is performed mainly in families where there are twins or multiple deliveries; children who are born with the placenta, children who are born with the legs first,[44] and children who are generally stubborn. It is usually handed down from person to person. Before a home is opportuned to have one, any elderly person in the community who can perform the rite is invited to come and assist in instituting it. During this period, the mother of the house may be initiated towards the end of the ceremony so that she can take over the celebration.

The basic requirements for this sacrifice are as follows: two clay pots (these pots are called the "Ikeng") two calabashes with trimmed edges, (referred to as the "agheyn"), four snail shells and a small grinding stone. These essential items make up the body of the ikeng. When the time of the ritual approaches, which is usually when the moon is appearing in the sky, the person to perform the rite prepares corn beer. Initially, this corn beer was prepared about three days to the day of the ritual. In modern times, it is prepared on the day of the ritual. After cooking of the corn beer, the celebrant proceeds to look for herbs that are required. (locally listed as nshim, ilol, fiwayn, cha'cha', mighayn and fisus fi ngang). Among the above listed herbs, some like (fiwuyn, nshim, fisus fi ngang , cha' cha') are ground and mixed with castor oil while other herbs are mixed with water in the 'agheyn" and used for bathing. 'Afi atita" is usually used to anoint the "ikeng" and the upper frame of the door at the entrance to the ritual room. Hence, any house that has the ikeng can easily be identified owing to these three marks on the doorpost. The three marks are white in colour.

When all the herbs have been gathered, the person proceeds to grind egusi and corn fufu. Dry fish, preferably tilapia is used to prepare egusi pudding. After all the above preparations have been made, the ikeng is removed from where it usually rests and placed on the ground. The ati abayn is ground, mixed with water, and then used to anoint the ikeng and doorframe. The prepared corn beer, usually in a calabash locally called 'mboh' is taken to the door by the celebrant. She then proceeds to sprinkle quantities of it beginning from the entrance towards the inner section of the house while saying the following words:

> "O gods, stand at the door and take this child's corn beer.
> Good god should take through the mouth
> While the bad one takes through the nose."

After this recitation, she proceeds to fill the ikeng with the corn beer. The shells of the snail are put into the ikeng at this moment. After the preparation of fufu and egusi, the celebrant cuts a large piece of fufu, places it on her palms, and places a small amount of egusi on top of the fufu. She then proceeds to the door, breaks a small portion of the fufu and places some of the egusi on it. After this, she says

> "O gods, stand at the door and take this child's fufu.
> The good god should take through the mouth
> While the bad one takes through the nose."

After these words are spoken, she proceeds to throw the small portion of food towards the door. From here, she turns towards the four corners of the house, repeats the same procedure with the fufu and egusi, but at this moment, she says:

> "O gods stand at the corners of this house and take this child's fufu.
> The good god should take through the mouth
> While the bad one takes through the nose."

After this, she throws small portions of the fufu to the four corners of the house. Then she turns and faces the ikeng itself, here she does a similar thing with the fufu and says

> "If the god of the child has hidden any where,
> Let him come and eat only under this ikeng iwayn."

Here, she throws the small portion of the fufu under the ikeng. Finally, she turns and faces the fire and repeats the same action with the fufu and then says:

> "All would be gathered and given to you Kwifon" and then the small portion of the fufu would be thrown into the fire.

When the above rituals have been performed, someone else in the room moves over to the celebrant, and collects the fufu from her hand and then proceeds to distribute it to all present. Those whose families do not offer such rituals are advised not to take part in the eating. It is believed that if they do, it will affect them ill.

This illness can only be cured if the Ikeng is instituted in the homes of the victims. This is another reason why this ritual is found in some homes.

After eating, some of the fufu is placed on the brim of the Ikeng and small amount of incense is placed on it and lit. This is done on two adjacent points only, on each of the ikeng. The occupants are then called to come and bask themselves in the smoke of the incense. This basking is closely followed by drinking corn beer but before this, the celebrant goes to the Ikeng, removes the 'ngôlsi' (shells of snails), and places them back again. If they sink and all do rise pointing upwards, it means there is a fault somewhere or misfortune is looming around the corner. If the fault cannot be discerned by the celebrant, all she needs to do is say: "o god whatever it is, forgive me for I do not know."

After these words, the 'ngôlsi' would then take their expected positions and drinking commences. This is done in order of seniority beginning from the eldest to the youngest of those present.

When drinking is over, if the rite requires that someone should be initiated, this takes place at this moment. The celebrant calls the person, hold the person's hands, and dip them in the ikeng. The individual then removes some of the corn beer from the Ikeng using the ngôlsi and may either drink or give it to someone else in the house. This marks the end of the initiation process. The individual is now given the right to send her hands in the Ikeng and give corn beer to any other person. It should be noted that anyone who is not initiated has no right to remove corn beer from the Ikeng.

Bathing follows immediately after this. Bathing can be done either thoroughly or partially depending on the individuals. Herbs that were selected, ground and mixed with castor oil are used to anoint those present. Some of the ilôl is wrapped around the neck of the participants. Ikeng is decorated with ilôl and anointed.

At this moment, the sacrifice is over and the Ikeng is left on the floor for three days before it is taken away to its place to wait for the next moon to show up in the sky, which would bring about the next rite to be performed. However, if a family fails to perform the rite regularly, children will be frequently sick and the only remedy for the sickness would be to perform the rite.

The above description is based mainly on the ordinary celebrations. Such rites may be performed for special reasons such as for twins or children who show signs of abnormal behaviour or for the deaf. In any of these cases, some slight modifications are made. For those who fall in the category of twins, during preparation, salt, peeled dry corn and two stems or peace plants are added. After the victims have bathed and anointed themselves, everybody in the house moves up towards the Ikeng, takes the two peace plants, and then proceeds to beat the victims from head to toe while reciting the following: "Transform only to a green snake." The reason for choosing a green snake rather than any other reptile is that it is able to move fast and escape from impending danger. Green snakes traditionally are not to be killed. When one encounters one, one is expected not to harm it, for it may be someone's child. After the individual finishes performing the act, he/she places the peace plants on the ground with one corn and then goes away with another corn. This procedure is followed by all present in the house and at the end; the salt is distributed to the gods as it is said customarily. These gods are those who have partaken in the rite. This signals the end of the rite.

As concerns the deaf, what is needed in addition is an "ambah" and two small pieces of peace plants. After the usual procedure for the performance of the rite is over, the celebrant moves over to the victim, cuts and chews some alligator pepper. She splashes the juice in her mouth into the individual's ear once, plays the "ambah" twice, which produces the sound "chaka-chaka." The ambah is held against the two peace plants in both hands. She hits the individual's head and the ground saying "Be able to hear" This procedure is repeated three times. Only the celebrant performs the rite.

The main function of this ritual is healing. Apart from the above cited examples of some of the sicknesses it heals, it also helps in the case of twins where one is unable to walk. In such a situation, towards the end of the normal celebration, the child is beaten by everyone in the house using peace plants. At the end, the celebrant ties the ilôl on the child's neck and attaches it to the foot.

Not every child present eats of the special loaf and not every child drinks from the snail shell. Only children who have undergone the ritual may take part. A piece from the loaf of fufu is preserved for those who are away or are unavoidable absent. It is performed by women.

The Ikeng is a symbolic tradition that Kom people perform once a year. At the beginning, it was a means of bringing the family members together and as time went on it became tradition. It should be noted that not all families carry out this tradition. It is hereditary and some families have abandoned the practice because of Christianity and the influence of Western Culture. Some families have varying items such as the type of herbs and drinks used in the process, which may be corn beer or palm wine. Anyone may take part, but some families insist that only children whose families have may take part. In some cases, it is believed that there are certain children who are already members through the right of Ancestors. The Ikeng is performed in Kom to shower blessings on family members. Once the rite is over, the food is considered sacred. It must be eaten and care must be taken to make sure that it is not wasted. Those who are not around may have their share taken to them or preserved for them. The burning of incense is believed to keep evil spirits away.

Ise

It is traditional communal medicine used to treat some skin diseases. It is also used to bless the people and land to be productive during the planting season. This is the reason why its outing is usually at the threshold of the dry season and in March every year when farms have already been prepared for planting.

ORIGIN AND PURPOSE

Traditionally, it is believed that the kom people started this communal traditional form of healing when they settled in the present geographical location, one of the Fons instituted it when he introduced the custom of blessing the people and their farms. Another school of thought holds that it was a notable who had settled among the people of kom, because of the expansion through warfare and conquest of the local inhabitants and the hegemony of the kom people, who introduced it. Those who came to kom land through conquests were absorbed together with their traditions and customs, which were gradually accepted by the kom people. Many people of kom origin were attracted to these forms of healing and soon it spread all over the entire tribe. Today these can be found in places such as Fuli, Mbam, Mentang, and Fundong itself. All these shrines perform the same functions of healing of skin diseases, blessing of the land and the people at the beginning of the dry and rainy seasons.

INITIATION AND PURPOSE

On the eve of the traditional outing of the team, the members of the group, usually men who have been initiated and those to be initiated all come together. For one to become a member one needs to go through the initiation rite. Initiation takes the form of swearing in when one decides voluntarily to be initiated into the circles of this group. Those to be initiated are required to bring along a fowl and one bottle of castor oil on the day of initiation. When the day is at hand and the ceremony begins, the person concerned stands at the entrance to the shrine. The eldest person or the leader, usually the Quarter Head comes to meet the person at the entrance of the shrine with a spear. The person holds the spear on one end while the leader holds it on the other end. In this way, he is led into the shrine where the rite of initiation is performed. It should be noted that all medicines needed for the outing are prepared the previous day. When the person to be initiated is in the shrine, his fowl is killed and the blood rubbed all round the Iweng together with Castor. During this period, the one initiated sits on the stone. The stone is of significance. When the chief dies, this stone is turned upside down and no activity takes place during that time. When a new chief takes over, he comes and overturns the stone to its normal position. A fowl and Fufu corn are prepared on that day and the eldest person of the ise brings the chief, who is the leader and instructs him on what usually happens and his role in the ise.

No woman is allowed to take part. Before eating, the chief celebrant, usually the Quarter Head or the eldest person blesses the food. The blessing is done in this way; he takes the food and speaks to the ancestors, saying that: 'may the good ones take by the mouth and the bad ones take by the nose, and while talking, he throws some food round as said in the Iking. No one may take the fowl home for whatever reason. Here, one may not complain about what is given him. A member may not fight or quarrel with another member. One may not steal or make false accusations against another member.

The Dynamics and Contradictions of Evangelisation in Africa

Members of the Ise on one of their outings. On the right one of the indigenes receiving some of their concoctions usually administered during their outings.

The person who brings an initiate or the eldest member appoints someone to teach the initiate the regulations and the type of herbs required as well as the mode of preparation.

The new member is handed over to someone who will school him on the rules and regulations of the ise. One may not talk to another or urinate with the iweng in his hand. If one wants to urinate or talk, the iweng must be placed on the ground. When one is on the way one may talk only to members of the ise or the children with whom one works. Before one talks to another be it one of the members or children with whom one is working, one must put the iweng on the ground. After the initiation is done, the fowl is cooked and only members of the ise may eat. Once this initiation is over and outing is around the corner, the men involved take care to make sure that the right herbs are harvested.

On the day of the outing, two or more ise members, accompanied by helpers, make the rounds in the villages and quarters. On approaching, every person is required to avail himself for this medication. It is administered with a peace plant which is used to smear the portions prepared with castor oil on the chests of the recipients. No one may receive this concoction with shoes on or with jewellery on.

Occasionally, women and children avail themselves by going to the shrines themselves to be bathed. On such a visit, one is expected to come along with a bottle of castor oil and a calabash for water. Traditionally, the purpose of the ise is to bless the farms during the planting seasons and to prevent the malevolent actions of spirits, witches, and wizards by preventing them from destroying the crops in the farms. This is to forestall the possibility of shortage of food, which is a recipe for famine. This is the reason why peace plants used are kept around the farms in the villages. Communally and medically, it is used to treat people who are suffering from scabies. When the Fon passes away, all the ise in kom go to the palace at Laikom and remain there until the last day of the celebration. Here they wash and bless the people. Some of these ise are male while others are female.

AFRICAN SPIRITUAL WORLD, SICKNESS, HEALING AND THE TEACHING OF THE CHURCH

The African spiritual world is present to people in their daily life. The spirits of the departed ones are much around. When misfortune strikes and the cause cannot be immediately identified among the community of the living, then the world of the departed becomes a likely source. The blame is often placed on the spirit of the departed for any misfortune if the cause cannot be found among the living. The spirits of the departed relative can be malevolent or peaceful.

The good spirit of a departed may give warning signals before executing the malevolent act and will only act only if the surviving relative remains adamant or intransigent. The evil spirit of the departed relative may strike without warning and often in a lethal manner. For the African, the ancestors are the guardians of the family but also the source of misfortune if not appeased ritually in sacrifice.

Over the centuries, heretics and saints alike were associated with devils in one way or another. The church in the past was associated with Witchcraft accusations and burning of witches. In the 1960's the thoughts and preoccupation with demons was no longer the main worry of most people in Europe. Europe preoccupied itself with science and not with superstitious hangovers of the mediaeval age. Though holding in an age of science and relativism, The Second Ecumenical Vatican Council did not allow this issue of the presence of spirits, demons, and evil spirits to go unattended. The mind of the church regarding this benign and paranormal issue of demons and evil spirits was articulated in this document. *Christian Faith and Demonology*, states that: we repeat, therefore that, though still emphasizing in our day the real existence of the demonic, the Church has no intention either of taking us back to the dualistic and Manichaean speculations of the past or proposing an alternative explanation more acceptable to reason. Its desire is simply to remain faithful to the gospel and its requirements. To sum up: The position of the Catholic Church on demons is clear and firm. The existence of Satan and the demons has indeed never been the subject of an explicit affirmation by the magisterium but this is because the questions have never been put in those terms. Heretics and Faithfuls alike, on the basis of scripture were in agreement on the existence of the chief misdeeds of Satan and his demons.[45]

The challenges, which are related to the devil, the means of healing and warding off misfortune, are not new. Already, St. Augustine could tell the Christians of his time "Brothers, it happens that a temptation from the side of the devil comes to a sick person, telling him/her; 'if only you had consulted that medicine man, you would already be cured", or: "if only you had applied those charms, you would already be restored to your health." If you give in to the tempter, you have offered sacrifice to the Devil. But if you disdain him, you have earned a martyr's crown. Maybe someone comes and tells you to send your belt, or a piece of your clothing to a certain diviner, so that he may diagnose what measures you are to take for your cure, or whether you will escape your bout of sickness. Or someone else may counsel you to see that famous doctor, expert in smoking out spirits, who has the reputation of having healed whoever has seen him, and had proved able to stop any vexation in the home of his patients."

For St. Augustine, such persons had violated their baptismal vows! The devil likes to deceive negligent and lukewarm Christians. If for instance a case of theft has occurred, that cruel persecutor suggests to your friends the insinuation "Come secretly to a certain place where I will provide you a person able to reveal to you the thief of your money! But when you reach the diviner's place, do on no account acknowledge yourself to be a Christian!" – now you see what wickedness lukewarm Christians can be lured into, who are not ashamed to commit such sacrilege only in order to recover their temporary wealth. They should never doubt that thereby they have disowned Christ and have aligned themselves again with the Devil.

He warned his Christians in words that are very relevant to us today. It also happens that women persuade themselves to provide their sick children with an amulet, which is contrary to Catholic faith. This is a temptation from the part of the devil. People go to sacred springs and trees, they make use of amulets, and cut tattoos into their skin, they frequent medicine men and diviners when they fall sick. How much better and healthier would it be for them if they ran to Church for the Eucharist and the holy oil, to anoint in all confidence themselves and their dear ones! Then according to the saying of James the Apostle not only would they receive health of the body, but also remission of sin, for through him the Holy Spirit made the promise: "if anyone among you is sick, let him call the presbyters of the Church … and his sins will be forgiven him."

The Church in its sacramental life has never ceased to acknowledge the reality of the demon and his ability to harm a person from the rite of Christian initiation of Adults to liturgy of the sick. The acknowledgement of the subtle works of the evil one, have not escaped the attention of the celebration of the Church. However, a careful reading of the document shows how the Church had to walk the tight rope to prevent itself from falling off to any of the two extremes.

THE SACRAMENTAL RITES
RITE OF CHRISTIAN INITIATION OF ADULTS AND DEMONOLOGY

The Council was very keen not to say too little or to give away too much. On demons and exorcism, the fathers of the council were very careful not to be seen as amplifying what was seen as a hangover of the middle ages or falling prey to the relativism and scientific teaching which not only rejected the teachings that touch on demons as superstition but also rejected the gospel as out of touch. The once striking pronouncement was gradually toned down to reflect the current thinking. It is true enough that the rite of Christian initiation of adults has been altered and no longer addresses commands to the devil. It achieves the same purpose, however, by turning to God in prayer. The language is now less striking but it is nonetheless expressive and effective. Consequently, it is an error to claim that exorcisms have been eliminated from the new ritual of Baptism. The error is, in fact, perfectly obvious since the new rite for the catechumenate has even introduced hitherto unknown 'minor' exorcism throughout the period of the catechumenate, before the 'major' exorcisms.[46]

Writing on Exorcisms in the Baptismal Rite, the council states that exorcisms remain, then, now, as in the past, they ask for victory over 'Satan', 'the devil', 'the prince of this world' and 'the power of darkness', while the three traditional 'scrutinies', during which the exorcisms take place, as in the past, have the negative and positive aims they always had. To free the catechumens from sin and the devil, and at the same time, to strengthen them in Christ, the rite of infant Baptism, too, whatever people may think still has an exorcism. This does not mean that the Church considers these children to be possessed by Satan: the Church does, however, believe that they, too, need all the effects of the redemption wrought by Christ. Before baptism, every man, child or adult, bears the mark of sin and Satan's action.

On the Liturgy of Penance and Liturgy of the Sick the council states that the liturgy of private penance has less to say of the devil today than in the past. On the other hand, communal penance services have brought back an old prayer, which mentions the influence of Satan on sinners. In the ritual of the sick, as we have already pointed out, the prayer in the Recommendation of the Departing Soul of God no longer emphasizes the disquieting presence of Satan. In the course of the anointing, however, the celebrant prays that the sick person 'be freed from sin and every temptation.' The sacred oil is regarded as a 'protection for body, soul, and spirit, and the prayer Commendo te without mentioning hell and the devil, indirectly refers to their existence and action when it asks Christ to save the dying person and number him or her among 'his' sheep and 'his' chosen ones. The language used is evidently intended to avoid upsetting the sick person and his family but it derives nevertheless from faith in the mystery of evil.

In other periods of history, men were certainly somewhat naïve in expecting to meet one or another demon at the crossroads of their minds. But would it not be just as naïve today to assume that our mind is where the relations between soul and body, between the supernatural, the preternatural and the human, and between revelation and reason all intertwine? These matters have always been regarded as vast and complicated. Our contemporary methods, like those of earlier generations, have insurmountable limitations. Modesty, which, after all, is a characteristic of true intelligence, must always have a place and help us keep to the right path. This virtue takes account of the future and enables the Christian to make room for the contribution of revelation, or, to put it in a single word, for faith.[47]

The council finally concluded that evil is a mystery. It is certain that the reality of the devil, as concretely attested by what we call the mystery of evil is today, as always, an enigma surrounding the Christian's life. We are little wiser than the Apostles as to why the Lord permits it and how he makes it serve his purposes. Yet, it may be that in our civilization, which is so secularized and so focused on the horizontal plane of man's life, unexpected manifestations of this mystery have a meaning not impossible to ascertain. For, such manifestations oblige us to look further and higher, beyond immediate evidences. The insolent threats with which evil darkens our path enable us to glimpse the existence of a realm beyond which challenges us to understand it and then turn to Christ so that we may hear from him the Good News of the salvation he graciously offers us.[48]

THE CHURCH'S FAITH IN HEALING TODAY

The early Church not only believed in divine healing but also prayed for God to work miracles of healing. What does the Church believe about divine healing today? The simplest and most direct way to answer this question is to examine how the Church prays for healing in her prayers, especially in the liturgy. The principle is this: if the Church prays for something in the liturgy, she believes that her request is according to the mind of God, and therefore, are an immediate source for studying the faith of the Church.[49]

Pope Pius XII in his great encyclical letter, Mediator Dei, said, The entire liturgy has the Catholic faith for its content, in as much as it bears public witness to the faith of the Church. For this reason whenever there was a question of defining a truth revealed by God, the sovereign Pontiff and the Councils in their recourse to the theological sources, as they are called, have drawn many an argument from this sacred science of the Liturgy. For an example in point, our predecessor of immortal memory, Pius IX so argued when he proclaimed the Immaculate Conception of the Virgin Mary. Similarly, during the discussion of a doubtful or controversial truth, the Church and the Holy Father have never failed to look to the age-old and time-honoured sacred rites for enlightenment.

In 1956, Pius XII said: It would be very difficult to find one truth of the Christian faith which is not expressed in some way in the liturgy. In the liturgy, the Church communicates abundantly the treasures of the deposit of faith, of the truth of Christ. To find out what the Church believes, we must study her prayers. This study is open to all the faithful. Anyone who can pray the prayers of the Church can ask, what does the Church mean in this prayer? This will be our approach in the rest of this book. We will look at the prayers of the liturgy, the prayers that the Church says in her sacraments, and what we ask for in this prayer or in this sacrament.[50]

In The Constitution on the Sacred Liturgy, the Second Vatican Council tells us: The liturgy is the outstanding means by which the faithful can express in their lives, and manifest to others, the mystery of Christ and the real nature of the true Church (No. 2)The prayers of the liturgy manifest our faith in God. In our prayers, we ask God for strength in our weakness, healing in our sickness, forgiveness in our sinfulness, joy in our sorrows, and light in our darkness. We pray to be filled with the Spirit, to be filled with the power of his gifts. These prayers reveal our God. Our God is a God who saves, who heals and delivers from evil, who comforts, enlightens and strengthens his people. That is the God we worship, and those are the blessings we ask from our God. If, in the sacred moment of liturgical worship, the Church prays to the Father in the name of Jesus for health of mind and body, for deliverance from evil, and for joy in sorrows, we know that request is in accordance with God's will. We know that the Church, because she makes this request believes in divine healing. The answer to the question, does the Church believe in divine healing? Must be an emphatic yes, and the reason we give is this: throughout her liturgical worship, the Church keeps praying for health of mind and body.[51]

FERTILITY RITES

Kom people attach a lot of importance to farming, partly because the tribe derives its livelihood from agriculture. They are agriculturally oriented due to the absences of natural or man made resources. In face of climatic hazards such as destructive strong winds, and invasion of the farms by pest, people have certain rites and rituals which they believed are capable of forestalling these eventualities. Farming the mainstay of the people is regulated by the executive arm of the Fon - the Kwifon. Kwifon is responsible for warning people against impending famine, taking measures to ensure food security as well as performing annual fertility rites. There are three main fertility rites in Kom. These rites are Fichwo, Ngoesi and Ngyvn.

The application of these fertility rites usually begins in March shortly after the onset of the rainy season. This period of rites is ushered in by the traditional communal hunting usually during the month of April. This is done by all the adult males of every village. Originally, the aim was to hunt down all wild animals which were dangerous to human beings or destructive to crops. Presently these animals are taken to the palace where each village is expected to bring at least one or more animals.

Thereafter, the rite of the Ngoesi (blessing of the seeds is performed at Laikom shortly after the communal hunting exercise for the Fon. This act is actually done at (isoh) a place in Laikom constructed for that purpose. This is performed by selected Kom notables and some members of the Kwifon. The piece of land is cleared and ridges are made. Guinea Corn and other crops in Kom are mixed and planted. After one week the elders inspect the nurseries personally and ascertain for themselves the outcome of their exercise and what has transpired in the nurseries. If birds eat up the corn and other plants, it is an indication that good days lie ahead and vice versa. The Fon's farm is cleared in preparation for planting. This is done by the Achàef family and completed by the Kwifon. When birds eat up the seeds it signifies a good harvest. For the purpose of simplicity we will limit our analysis to one.

These rites are mostly done on itu-ikijem and itu-a-bum which are Kom working days. The Fichwo in Kom is a traditional fertility rite which is performed yearly as the other above. Fichwo follows ngoesi immediately. This has taken place since the arrival and settlement of the Kom people, it is mostly ceremonial. This also takes place at Laikom in a specific place. Once the rites have been performed certain conditions relating to weather are expected. Thunder, lighting and prolonged rains are the usual signs expected in the days after the rites. The following rules are observed by the community. Beginning with the day after the ritual no sound of drumming is to be heard any where in kom; no death is to be celebrated, no firing of gunshots and no building of houses is permitted.

The reason for this is simple. The ancestors of Kom who are believed to oversee and moderate the rhythm of every facet of life in Kom land are appeased by offering sacrifice on the graves at Laikom. Strong winds are usually attributed to witches and wizards. Here, the gods are appeased in order to keep a tight rein on their malevolent activities mainly through destructive strong winds. Once this is done there are heavy winds the following day with rains to signal that the ancestors have accepted the sacrifices. These winds indicate that there will be no heavy winds during the year. If there are no winds it is a bad sign. It means that strong winds during the year. The sacrifices were not well offered and therefore heavy rains and winds will come.

Another fertility rite in Kom is ngyvn. This is done in almost all the villages. It should be noted that this is the only fertility rite that is performed at the village level. Here, anyone who wishes to become a member can ask to be initiated. In each village there is a compound where this rite is performed, it can be the oldest compound or the village head's compound. It is done by selecting herbs; specific herbs known only to its members. This concoction is poured out on road junctions in selected places. No one is allowed to watch when the rites are person or members are in action at road junctions and selected sacred places. The central rite of this fertility rite is simple but rich in mystery.

The rite is meant to prevent witches and wizards who move in strong winds with diabolical aims of destroying crops. It should be noted that during the months of June and July in Kom there are strong winds which are attributed to these malevolent witches and wizards whose main aim is to destroy crops. In this light, ngyvn acts as a deterrent to their malevolent actions. This is why it is applied on road sides, road junctions, roundabouts and farms and at times at the doors of individuals in the village, to prevent evil people from destroying crops and property.

FERTILITY RITES IN THE ANCIENT NEAR EAST

Fertility rites are not a preserve of the kom people. All over the grass field area, many ethnic groups if not all have fertility rites. Fertility rites go beyond age and time. The ancient tribes of the Near East made use of even more outrageous fertility rites suited for their time and age. Archeological evidence has proven that sacred prostitution was a form of their fertility rite. "The discovery of the ugaritic tablets in 1929 has given us a good idea of the myths and rites used by the Canaanites. Both involve generous amounts of magical imitation in which priests and worshippers represent sexual mating of gods. One example would be the annual New Year Festivals in which the king of Baal's representative would unite himself with a priestess in sacred prostitution to guarantee the land's prosperity and fertility of the coming year. At the same time, worshippers abandoned themselves to sexual license with official cult prostitutes, both men and women, in order to fulfill prayers and vows asking for children or better crops or an end to drought[52].

Even the Jewish Passover feast had its roots in a pagan rite of fertility. Originally, a young animal was sacrificed to obtain fertility for the whole flock and the blood was put on tent poles to drive way evil powers. This ritual has all the appearance of a rite celebrated when the tribe broke camp to head for the fresh spring pastures.

Only with time did Israel give it a new meaning which finally culminated in the final Passover in which our Passover lamb was sacrificed. Even Israel was tempted continuously by this seductive fertility rite of the Canaanites.

While the Church has no official fertility rite today, Christians no doubt have adopted the practice of blessing their seeds before planting in Church. One cannot completely escape this flurry of sacrifices offered at the level of the community for fertility of the soil. It is left to the Church to come up with more appropriate rites to make it more significant.

TRADITIONAL DAYS OF OBLIGATIONS
ORIGIN AND PURPOSE

In Kom there are only two days of obligation, they are Itu I iyv+n+kom and itu+bol in their eight days cycle. It is believed that when kom people settled on their present site under the leadership of Jinabo I the next day was declared a day of rest because they had moved over long distances and that day became a day of rest called in Kom language as +tui+bol, meaning resting day. In addition, in Kom, this day has also been set aside as a day when cultural and social activities are performed. It is fondly called country Sunday.

The +tuiyvn+kom is another day of obligation in Kom land. This day came into being when the first Fon of Kom died and was buried on Itu Ktjem. The next day which was Itu'iyvintkom was declared a day of mourning for their Fon, and the day came into existence. The day became a traditional day in respect of the first Fon of Kom. In kom these are the fourth and the eight day. Different theories point to the origin of these days. The first theory points to the origin of the fourth day (The Itu'iyvin+kom) as the day when kom people were burnt alive in their houses at Babessi. While the eight day (+tui+bol) was a day of rest from the busy week of negotiation with the people of Bum and Banbaki over the paying of tributes. These days are also considered in Kom as days when ancestors visit farms and bless the crops. In kom, it is taboo for someone to farm on these days; women and men stay at home or occupy themselves with other activities. Today many Kom cultural activities such as death celebrations and other activities of social life take place on these days. In the early days of Christianity, no direct attempts were made to violate it. It was a day set aside for doctrine classes and other Church activities. Even today, 'country Sunday' as it is called, is used by the Church for activities which Christians would otherwise not attend because of farming. The African Christian ends up giving to Baal what belongs to Baal and to Yahweh what belongs to Yahweh.

CHRISTIAN DAYS OF OBLIGATION
ORIGIN AND PURPOSE

Christianity like other religions has its own days of obligation. The Christian day of obligation has its roots in the Jewish religion. The important holy days in the calendar of ancient Israel were the three pilgrimage feasts (unleavened bread, Weeks, and tabernacles) and the Passover. The Passover was to be celebrated in conjunction with the full moon of the first month; each family was to select an unblemished, male, one-year-old lamb. At twilight on the 14th (Exodus 12:6: "between the two evenings"), the lamb was slaughtered and the blood sprinkled on the lintels and doorposts of the house. During this night of the full moon, the lamb was roasted and eaten; not one of its bones was to be broken, and whatever was left over after the meal had to be eaten also, and those who partook of the meal had to be dressed as if ready for a journey. In case a family was too small to consume a whole lamb, it joined some neighbours. Slaves and resident aliens could take part, so long as they were circumcised.

On the 15th of the month, the weeklong feast of Unleavened Bread began. All leftover leavened bread had to be destroyed and for the following week, only unleavened bread could be eaten. The first and seventh days of the festival were holidays on which religious gatherings took place. The role the Sabbath played in Israelite life and thought made it quite unique. It was not just a holiday on which to rest up from another week of work. It was related to the covenant that God had made with his people and was a day consecrated to him in a special way.

In the early days, however, the Sabbath was a joyful, relaxed holiday, predominantly religious but not overly restrictive. Manual labour and business were suspended, but the people could move about freely. They made pilgrimages to nearby sanctuaries (Isa 1:13;

Hos 2: 13) or went to consult their prophets (2Kgs 4:23). Then during the exile, when celebration of the other feasts was impossible, the Sabbath came into prominence as the distinctive sign of the covenant. After the exile, although the Sabbath continued to be a day of pleasurable relaxation, it was subject to tighter restrictions. All business and travel were forbidden (Isa 58: 13); the people could not carry anything from their homes or do any work (Jer 17:21-22, a postexilic addition). During his second visit to Jerusalem, Nehemiah reacted vigorously to the people's neglect of the Sabbath laws by ordering the city gates closed and extracting a promise of future fidelity. However, with the coming of Christianity and Sunday events equally changed. It was not a national holiday as it is today but only for a minority who were Christians.

TRADITIONAL CONCEPT AND PRACTICE OF JUSTICE

Traditionally the people have always had a judicial system, which meted out punishment on defaulters. These forms of justice were administered at all levels of the society, from the executive arms of the Fon, to the village level. Some of them included trial by ordeal, execution, ostracisation, placement of injunction on particular compounds and placement under house arrest of certain individuals who had committed certain abominations down to simple fines. However, we will concentrate on the feminine wing of the kom judicial system. The reason is simple. It is one of the first instances in which early Christianity was entangled. Like all aspects of culture, anlu was borne out of necessity to protect womanhood long before western feminism began to raise eyebrows. The Anlu, which means 'to drive away', is a women's organization, whose goal is to redress crimes committed against womankind, especially with obscene reference to their private.[53]

The origin of Anlu is narrated by Kom's oral tradition. The Kom people used to pay annual tribute to the chiefdom of Menjang (a neighbouring tribe) in the form of building a house. The Kom Fon got tired of the tribute levy and advised his people to resent paying it. The Menjang people interpreted the resentment of the Kom people to pay them tribute as an act of rebellion and decided to punish them accordingly. They secretly planned a punitive expedition against the Kom people when the men would have gone out on a hunting expedition and it leaked to the queen mother through her network of spies. The queen mother mobilized the women, disguised them as men by putting on their husbands' attires. Anlu came to be recognized as a reputable organization for handling women and state affairs. It is, in essence, a disciplinary traditional organisation, with a military and a mythical origin for the defence of the right of women and the state.

The assertion that in time of crisis the African seeks refuge in his time-honoured traditions came true in kom in the late 1950's. These traditions of redress were not Christian at all. However, in time of crisis the Christian women at Njinikom without qualms resorted to what would have been considered repugnant. Over the years, the Mill Hill Missionaries had introduced the liberal ideas of individual freedom, Christian morality, social justice, through doctrine classes, the convents, Health Clinics, and more formally through their educational institutions. However, the obtrusive manner in which the missionaries inculcated the theory and practice of human rights and justice and for which they were detested by the Traditional and Colonial Authorities was when they publicly defended their Christians and catechists in open courts and tended to ridicule and belittle the chiefs and the natives laws as it were.[54]The Mill Hill missionaries themselves were soon to have the taste of their medicine when in 1958 the Catholic women staged demonstrations all over the region.

This movement was massively led by Catholic Christian women. The cult became so ferocious in its activities that for close to three years not only Churches were boycotted but also schools, markets and government establishments to the extent that life and all development in the area were completely paralysed.[55] By 1961, all the Christians who had swelled the ranks of this movement even those in the forefront returned to the Church and to the sacraments. With hindsight, one can easily see how in time of social crisis African Christians can easily return to their roots by unearthing solutions to redress an injustice regardless of its variance with Christianity.

CONCLUSION

Did Christianity make any attempt at replacing what it had made incumbent on Africans to repudiate? Can the present crisis in African Christianity with many drifting towards syncretism be solely attributed to this creation of the vacuum? Did Christianity even make it incumbent on Africans to reject African customs in an all out manner? What is unchristian in African customs?

Christianity generally stands on four main poles. Christianity is celebrated in the liturgy through the sacraments. It is experienced and lived in the commandments and what is believes is found in the creed. All these are supported by prayer. African Traditional Religion has all these components. It has its commandments, its creed, its sacraments and its prayers. The difference is that it is not articulated in the writing as Christianity. Chrisitanity attempted to create a model Christian community. A miniature of an ideal Christian community was found in the Christian villages of Njinikom, Esu, Basseng, and Shisong. It was an attempt to shield the convert from the contamination he had left. This was done with the hope that a spilled over and snow ball effect will make the whole community Christian. In these communities all that was pagan was rejected and Christians began to imbibe a new spirit. The early convert who had been washed clean in the waters of Baptism was washed clean of all cultural trappings which were considered rightly or wrongly as pagan. Officially and institutionally Christianity made a conscious effort to replace all that was considered pagan with what was Christian.

Looking back at this experiment of Christian villages one can rightly say that the experiment ended in failure for none of these establishments lived up to the expectation of the missionaries. In all of them practices which were considered pagan became rife in the very life time of those who were the architects. Why this reversion? A fundamental cause, which perhaps is not easily evident, is that mission Christianity has not penetrated deep into African religiosity. Mission Christianity has come to mean for many Africans simply a set of rules to be observed, promises to be expected in the next world, rhythmless hymns to be sung, rituals to be followed and a few other outward things.[56]

Some have described Christianity as a religion "Which is locked up six days a week, meeting only for two hours on Sundays and perhaps once during the week. It is Christianity, which is active in a Church building. The rest of the week is empty. Africans, who traditionally do not know religious vacuum, feel that they don't get enough religion from this type of Christianity, since it does not fill up their whole life and they are complete foreigners in mission Churches. Furthermore, African Christians often feel complete foreigners in mission Churches. Much of formal Christianity is based on books but there are older Christians who do not read; the hymns are translated from European, English, and American versions and are sung to foreign tunes.

Worship in mission Churches is simply dull for most Africans. Independent Churches are an attempt to find 'a place to feel at home', not only in worship but also in the whole profession and expression of Christian faith. Beneath the umbrella of independent Churches, African Christians can freely shed their tears, voice their sorrows, present their spiritual and physical needs, respond to the world in which they live and empty their selves before God[57].

Christianity generally frowned only at those values that stood at odds with Christian values. Generally, African values which did not conflict with Christianity were left at the discretion of the new converts. However, some of them created an unfortunate precedence unconsciously escaping the attention of the missionaries themselves. For example observing the traditional days of obligation usually having religious connotations and undertones were left to persist without any attempt to say a word. In some Parishes it was used as a day of Christian doctrine. As a consequence Christians were in fact serving Baal and Yahweh in a subtle way simultaneously. Giving Baal what was his due without raising eyebrows. Non Christians and practitioners of African Traditional Religion seem to have reciprocated this show of goodwill from the Christians by refraining from some of their usual tasks on Sundays which were fixed and not rotatory as the eight day cycles. Was the adhering to these traditional days of obligation giving Baal what was his due quietly?

African Christianity flourished under very unique conditions. Colonisation in some cases was not sympathetic to the missionaries. Besides, the system of indirect rule relied heavily on the Fons who were not sympathetic to missionary endeavours. Christianity was bound to develop outside the institutions of the tribal settings. From the start Christianity was bound to develop as a parallel system. But one must not overlook the fact that Christianity was able to gain a foothold in ancient Roman Empire and to make Christian laws civil because of civil legislation. The milieu in which this tradition, took root, flourished and became mandatory was Christian. In a letter from Emperor Constantine to Elpidius on state recognition of Sunday rest, in 321 the emperor decried "All judges, city people and craftsmen shall rest on the venerable day of the sun. But those in the country may freely attend to agriculture, since it often happens that this is the most suitable day for sowing grain or planting vines, so that the opportunity afforded by divine providence may not be lost, for the right season is of short duration.[58] Nevertheless, on that pleasant and joyful festal day let all be allowed to perform manumission of slaves, setting them free, and the legal formalities for such are not forbidden.[59] This backup to Christianity provided by civil legislation was not only lacking but impossible to obtain at the dawn of the Christian era in Africa.

Did Christianity answer the basic needs of the African Christian? Historically, in the apostolic times people converted to Christianity as a result of its efficacy on shedding light on basic human questions. Evangelization, healing and casting out of demons were part of the same package given wholesale. Even the conversion of Ireland is according to legend due to the saint's ability to rid the island of snakes. Gradually the Middle Ages saw the enshrining of the Christian doctrine in dogma that had been built up carefully as a bulwark against heresy. The rites and rituals which took up almost a superstitious outlook in the Middle Ages for the Christians became just observances for some. At the dawn of evangelization real concerns were rejected as superstitious.

Did Africans convert to Christianity because of some internal weaknesses in their religion or deficiencies? Ordinary Africans saw little need for a new religion since they already perceived themselves as spiritually self-contained, in a life comprehensively regulated by custom and tradition. Although termed pagan, the Kom peopled followed a well-developed form of African Traditional Religion. Traditionally the Kom people have an organised set up of religious rites and rituals which were highly utilitarian in character with a complex set of beliefs and practices which made the group religiously self sufficient. The religious practices of the Christianity such as sacraments and days of obligation, rites of passage had their counterpart in the African traditional religious set up. Religiously speaking the new religion brought in its wake rituals that could find their own semblance in the African cultural and religious milieu. The concept and reasons for them were fundamentally different. In African Traditional Religion, there is a basic moral code similar to that found in the bible. The fundamental difference was in many cases the being invoked and the guarantor of the efficacy of the rite.

With Catholic theology carefully refined over time, enshrined in dogma and polished with the tools of Thomistic and Aristotelian philosophy, Christianity apparently seems to have been gradually dispossessed of its power and efficacy. Christianity will only speak to Africans if the Church can go back to its roots by centering its life and mission on Christ Jesus the lord, the one who is the beginning and the end, before whom every knee shall bow, in heaven on earth and under the earth and every tongue confess that Jesus Christ is lord to the glory of God the Father.

Christianity has always frowned at those practices of African Traditional Religion that were perceived to be at variance with Christianity; why have Christians continually returned to their roots in time of crisis? Africans have no doubts about the efficacy of their traditions. If they had any, they would long have said farewell to them. There are certain institutions in African Fondoms and kingdoms shrouded in mystery. However, their aim is mainly to warn people harbouring diabolic intentions, expose witches and wizards, safeguard the agricultural sector, and to keep away malevolent spirits. The Second Vatican Council, in considering the customs, precepts, and teachings of the other religions, teaches that "although differing in many ways from her own teaching, these nevertheless often reflect a ray of that truth which enlightens all men"[60] Can these be channels of God's grace to the people who do not profess the faith in Jesus explicitly? With respect to the way in which the salvific grace of God—which is always given by means of Christ in the Spirit and has a mysterious relationship to the Church

—comes to individual non-Christians, the Second Vatican Council limited itself to the statement that God bestows it "in ways known to himself." Theologians are seeking to understand this question more fully. Their work is to be encouraged, since it is certainly useful for understanding better God's salvific plan and the ways in which it is accomplished[61]. Catholicism has always maintained that there are seeds of the gospel in every culture. It equally holds that those who lived upright lives can be saved if they had no opportunity to listen to the gospel. Can the words of Paul at Athens be of any relevance here?[62] Some of these ceremonies celebrated with the sole aim of saving life are in the eyes of Christians a sin. The answer is not simple. Writing about the church and other religions the Congregation for the Doctrine of the Faith examines this complex issue. It states: "Certainly, the various religious traditions contain and offer religious elements which come from God, and which are part of what "the Spirit brings about in human hearts and in the history of peoples, in cultures, and religions" Indeed, some prayers and rituals of the other religions may assume a role of preparation for the Gospel, in that they are occasions or pedagogical helps in which the human heart is prompted to be open to the action of God. One cannot attribute to these, however, a divine origin or an *ex opere operato* salvific efficacy, which is proper to the Christian sacraments. Furthermore, it cannot be overlooked that other rituals, insofar as they depend on superstitions or other errors (cf. 1 Cor 10:20-21), constitute an obstacle to salvation"[63]. Any solution to such a benign and irksome problem must provide the solutions to the needs of the Christians and make life more comprehensible; provide the way, the truth and the life. This is the crux of the matter and the core of inculturation. Reflection is needed here not because Christianity has not found the answers but to articulate in a better way these solutions to the Christians. While there are areas that concern mainly the individual, inculturation must go beyond and include the community. This dialogue between African Traditional Religion and Christianity must be frank, sincere, and effective.

Notes

1. Kiggins Thomas, Maynoth Mission to Africa The story of St. Patrick's Kiltegan Gill and Macmillan 1991.
2. Cf Forristal (1990). Op. cit., p.111.
3. Oyono Ferdinand (), The Old Man and the Medal. African Writer Series, Heinemann 1969.
4. Verdzekov Paul(1977), Diocese of Bamenda : Policy Concerning the Use of Cameroonian languages in the liturgy and Catechetics, Bamenda.
5. Mongo Beti(), Poor Christ of Bomba African Writer Series, Heinemann page 189.
6. Ibid.
7. Ibid.
8. Verdzekov Paul (1977), Pastoral Letter on Supersition in Area in Mbuy Tatah, H., (1995) Shepherd on the Bamenda Highlands.
9. Forristal Desmod (1990). The Second Burial of Bishop Shanahan, Dublin, Veritas Publication.
10. Verdzekov Paul op. cit.
11. Ibid.
12. Ibid.
13. Alward Shorter (1975) African Christian Theology, London, Chapman, p. 10.
14. Okere, T,(1974) Culture and Religion, Owerri, Black Academy Press, pp. 44 – 4.
15. John Paul II (1995) Post-Synodal Apostolic Exhortation Ecclesia in Africa on the Church in Africa and its Evangelizing Mission towards the year 2000 no. 78.
16. Ibid.
17. Ibid.
18. Jesus Living in Mary (1984) Handbook of the Spirituality of St. Louis de Montfort Litchfield, CT Montfort Publications.
19. Ibid.
20. Mbiti J. S. op. cit. p. 3.

21. MBI, Thaddeus (2004), Ecclessia in Africa is Us, An attempt at Liturgical Inculturation for the Ecclesiastical Province of Bamenda, Impression AMA-CNC.
22. Mbi Thaddeus Ecclesia is Africa is us p.114-117.
23. Paul Verdzekov, Pastoral letter on Christian Cemeteries. Sunday, 25th October, 1981.
24. Cf Robert O'Neil (1991) Mission to the British Cameroons. Mission Book service.
25. J.S Mbiti (1969) African Religion and Philosophy .East African Educational Publishers.
26. Mformie Bobe nkfum Personal communication with the author April, 16 2010.
27. The word Juju has many meanings. It is n object used as a fetish, a charm, or an amulet in West Africa or a supernatural power ascribed to such an object or a style of Nigerian popular music featuring electric guitars and traditional drums. It used in this book to refer to masquerades even though some have supernatural powers ascribed to them.
28. Martin Nkafu Nkemnkia (1995) Africa Vitalogy, A step Forward in African Thinking, Paulines Publications Africa p 136-137.
29. Mbiti op. cit., p.5.
30. Cf Mbi op.cit.
31. Augustine on Food and Drink offered to the dead in Cleric Luigi, (ed) A Reader in Early Patristic Nairobi.
32. St. Augustine city of God 8:2 Concerning the Nature of Honour which Christians pay their Martyrs in Cleric Luigi,(ed) A Reader in Early Patristic Nairobi.
33. Milingo Emmanuel, The world in between Christian Healing and Struggle for Spiritual survival p.87.
34. Paul VI(1968) The Credo of the people of God.
35. Catechism of the Catholic Church no.958.
36. *Mformie Bobe nkfum April 16, 2010 in a correspondent with the author.*
37. 1Sam 28: 3-19.

38. Letter to Sister Bridgid in Forristal Desmond (1990) The second Burial of Bishop Shanahan, Dublin: Veritas Publications p304.
39. Mbiti J.S. op. cit.
40. Mbiti J. S. op. cit.
41. Sister Philomena Fox, Lord that I may see In Forristal Desmod (1990). The Second Burial of Bishop Shanahan, Dublin, Veritas Publication.
42. John Paul II, (1990) Encyclical letter Redemptoris Missio, The mission of the Redeemer. No.6.
43. Mbi op. cit.
44. Mbi cited op p 47.
45. Christian Faith and Demonology S.C.D.W., Les formes multiples de la superstition, 26 June, 1975 in Flannery Austin (2008) Vatican Council II, St. Paul Publication, New Delhi.
46. Ibid.
47. Ibid.
48. Ibid.
49. Jim McManus (1984) The Healing Powers of Sacraments. Ave Maria Press, Indiana.
50. Ibid.
51. Ibid.
52. Lawrence Boadt, Reading the Old Testament, An introduction, Paulist press, New York/ Mahwah, N.J 1984.
53. Ndi Anthony Mbunwe: 2005, op. cit.
54. Ndi Anthony Mbunwe: 2005, op. cit.
55. Ibid.
56. Mbiti cited op.
57. Mbiti cited op.
58. Constantine to Elidius on State recognition of Sunday Rest 7 March, 321. in Cleric Luigi, (ed) A Reader in Early Patristic Nairobi.
59. Constantine to Elidius on State recognition of Sunday Rest 3 July 321 in Cleric Luigi, (ed) A Reader in Early Patristic Nairobi.

60. Congregation for the Doctrine of the Faith :Declaration "DominusIesus": on the Unicity and Salvific Universality of Jesus Christ and the Church no. 8.
61. Ibid no.21.
62. God has overlooked the times when people did not know him, but now he commands all of them everywhere to turn away from their evil ways (Acts 18:31).
63. Congregation for the Doctrine of the Faith Cit.op.

SELECTED BIBLIOGRAPHY

ACHEBE, Chinua (1971), Arrow of God, Ibadan Heinemann.

ALEXANDER VI (1493), Papal Bull, Inter Caetera.

ATANG, Ade Luke (2000), The struggle for the Catholic priesthood, Macacos.

BENEDICT XV. (1919) Apostolic Letter Maximum Illud: on the Propagation of the Faith Throughout the world. Translated by Thomas J. M. Burke, SJ Washington, DC: National Catholic Welfare Office.

BILL, R Austin (1983), Austin's Topical history of Christianity, Tyndale Publishers, Inc pg. 95.

BOADT, Lawrence, (1984), Reading the Old Testament, An introduction, Paulist press, New York/ Mahwah N.J.

BOSCH, David J., (1991), Transforming Mission paradigm Shifts on Theology of Mission Orbis books New York.

CHILVER, Elizabeth M., (1963), Native Administration in the West Central Cameroons, 1920-1954.

COMBY, Jean () How to read Church History Volume I from the beginning to the fifteenth century.

CONGREGATION FOR THE DOCTRINE OF FAITH, (2000) Iesus Dominus, Declaration on the Unicity and Salvific Universality of Jesus Christ and the Church.

CONGREGATION FOR THE DOCTRINE OF THE FAITH, (2007) Responses to Some Questions Regarding Aspects of the Doctrine of the Church.

CONGREGATION FOR THE DOCTRINE OF THE FAITH. (2000) Doctrinal Note on some aspects of Evangelisation.

CONGREGATION OF THE DOCTRINE OF THE FAITH(2001)Commentary on the Notification of the Congregation for the doctrine of the faith regarding the book toward a Christian Theology of Religious pluralism by Father Jacques Dupuis, S.J. Constitutions of St. Joseph's Society for Foreign Mission, 1930.

FORRISTAL, Desmond (1990), The Second Burial of Bishop Shanahan. Dublin, Veritas Publication.

JOHN PAUL II (1990), Encyclical letter Redemptotoris Missio.

JOHN PAUL II, (1995), Post-Synodal Apostolic Exhortation Ecclesia in Africa on the Church in Africa and its Evangelizing mission towards the year 2000.

JOHN XXIII (1963) Address delivered on the first day of the Council in St. Peter's Basilica. SCHAFF, Philip History of the Christian Church, Volume IV: Mediaeval Christianity. A.D. 590.

JUMBAM, Kenjo (1080), The White man of God Ibadan Heinemann.

JURGENS, William, (1992), The Faith of Our Fathers Volume one Theological publications in India.

KIGGINS, Thomas (1991), Maynooth Mission to Africa: The story of St. Patrick's Kiltegan. Gill and Macmillan.

KOCH, Carol (1994), The Catholic Church, journey wisdom and mission. St. Mary's Press.

LAMONT, Jean what went wrong Vatican II.

LUIGI, Clerici (ed), A Reader in Early Patristic Nairobi.

MBI, Thaddeus (2004), Ecclessia in Africa is Us, An attempt at Liturgical Inculturation for the Ecclesiastical Province of Bamenda, Impression AMA-CNC.

MBITI, John (1969), African religions and philosophy, East African Educational Publishers.

MCMANUS, Jim (1984), The Healing Powers of Sacraments. Ave Maria Press, Indiana.

MILINGO, Emmanuel, The world in between Christian Healing and Struggle for Spiritual survival

MONGO, Beti (), Poor Christ of Bomba African Writer Series, Heinemann page.

MUSI, John Yonghabi, (1990), A Mission Boy From Nowhere to Somewhere. Copy Printing Technology Bamenda.

NDI, Anthony Mbunwe (1983), Mill Hill Missionaries and the State in Southern Cameroons, 1922-1962, London.

Selected Bibliography

NGOH, Victor Julius, (1987), Cameroon 1884 - 1985: A Hundred Years of History, Yaoundé.

NKEMNKIA, Martin Nkafu (1995), Africa Vitalogy, A step Forward in African Thinking, Paulines Publications Africa.

NKWI, Paul Nchoji (1976), Traditional Government and Social Change. A study of the political institutions among the Kom of the Cameroon Grassfields, Freibourg.

NKWI, Paul Nchoji (1989), German presence in the western Grassfields 1891-1913 A German Colonial Account, Leiden.

NKWI, Paul Nchoji (2002), The Catholic Church in Kom Njinikom Parish 1927-2002, ICCASSRT Monograph No. 5.

O'NEIL, Robert (1991), Mission to the British Cameroons. Mission Book service.

OCHIEND, Odiambo (1997) African Philosophy An introduction , Consolata Institute of Philosophy, Nairobi.

OKERE, T, (1974) Culture and Religion, Owerri, Black Academy Press

OYONO, Ferdinand (1968), The Old Man and the Medal. African Writer Series, Heinemann

PAUL VI (1968) The Credo of the people of God.

Paul; VI (1968), The credo of the people of God.

PIUS XII (1940), Encyclical letter Saeculo Exeunte Octavo, on the eighteen century of the independence of Portugal.

PIUS XII (1958), encyclical letter Ad Apostolorum Principis on communism and the Church in china

POPE PIUS IX, (1863), Promotion of false doctrines.

POPE PIUS XI, (1926), Encyclical on Catholic Missions Rerum Ecclesiae.

SECOND VATICAN COUNCIL (1968), Decree on the Mission Activity of the Church Ad Gentes Divinitus.

SECOND VATICAN COUNCIL, Dogmatic Constitution Lumen Gentium.

SHORTER, Alward (1975), African Christian Theology, London, Chapman.

Souvenir St. Gabriel's Parish Bafmeng. 1965-1990.

TATAH, Mbuy H., Encounter the Truth Jubilee Sermons of Archbishop Paul Verdzekov, Bamenda: Unique Printers.

The History of the Catholic Church in Fuli Kom, (2000) 1975-2000. A silver Jubilee publication Copy Printing Technology, Bamenda.

VERDZEKOV, Paul (1977), Diocese of Bamenda: Policy Concerning the Use of Cameroonian languages in the liturgy and Catechetics, Bamenda.

VERDZEKOV, Paul (1981), Pastoral letter on Christian Cemeteries, Bamenda.

VERDZEKOV, Paul (2004), Quinquinnial Report: Archdiocese of Bamenda: 1999-2004.

www.ingramcontent.com/pod-product-compliance
Lightning Source LLC
Chambersburg PA
CBHW021125300426
44113CB00006B/292